World Food for Student Cooks

Healthy, delicious, easy-to-make dishes for the food-truck-loving, noodle-slurping, taco-crunching, mac & cheese lover!

Krista McLellan, Rd

Formac Publishing Company Limited
Halifax

Formac Publishing Company Limited recognizes the support of the Province of Nova Scotia through Film and Creative Industries Nova Scotia. We are pleased to work in partnership with the Province of Nova Scotia to develop and promote our creative industries for the benefit of all Nova Scotians. We acknowledge the support of the Canada Council for the Arts, which last year invested $157 million to bring the arts to Canadians throughout the country.

Cover design: Meghan Collins
Cover image: Shutterstock & iStock

Library and Archives Canada Cataloguing in Publication
McLellan, Krista, author
      World food for student cooks : healthy, delicious, easy-to-make dishes for the food-truck-loving, noodle-slurping, taco-crunching, mac & cheese lover! / Krista McLellan.

Includes index.
ISBN 978-1-4595-0455-4 (paperback)

      1. International cooking. 2. Quick and easy cooking. 3. Cookbooks. I. Title.

TX725.A1M35 2016   641.59   C2016-902692-2

Formac Publishing Company Limited
5502 Atlantic Street
Halifax, Nova Scotia, Canada
B3H 1G4
www.formac.ca

Printed and bound in Canada.

To Andrew,
my loving
and gracious
taste tester.

Introduction

Worried you might not survive without home cooking?

Treating yourself to great restaurants and food trucks can be fun — and sometimes absolutely necessary — but it is far too indulgent for everyday eating. *World Food for Student Cooks* can help, with its collection of trendy recipes that fit into your student lifestyle.

Work happens around the clock, budgets are skin-tight, and it's all too easy for the Freshman 15 to turn into the Freshman 45. With this book, you will be empowered to make friends with food, save some money and improve your health by using these resources and finding your confidence in the kitchen. Notes on cooking techniques, tips on buying and storing food and simple tricks to keep trendy foods healthy will let you be successful at feeding yourself, whether you're on your own for the first or the thirty-first time.

I wrote this multicultural cookbook so students would be motivated to prepare fun and healthy meals at home more often. I was funded by student loans for far too many post-secondary years on my path to becoming a dietitian, and I know many of you suffer from the same struggles I faced as a student. Now I can help you avoid the dietary pitfalls of the student's journey into adulthood.

Throughout my education and early work as a dietitian, I developed relationships with people from around the world who shared their thoughts on what makes cultural cuisines special. You'll find the recipes in this book cover the globe: from home-cooked comfort foods to trendy fusion favourites. Most of these recipes are quick and easy, giving you the 101 in culinary skills for future adventures with food. And, even better, they won't break the bank.

With *World Food for Student Cooks*, you'll find yourself preparing meals and snacks that are flavourful, fun and nutritious — keeping you healthy for your busy life.

— Krista

Use this key to help you find recipes you'll love!

 Fast! These recipes can be made in less than half an hour, start to finish!

 Healthy! These are the recipes that will make your body happiest. We all need treats sometimes, though!

 Cost meter! $ is for under $10 and $$ is for under $20

 Food Truck Favourite! If you love eating from food trucks, chances are you'll love and recognize these favourites!

Contents

let's get you started and sorted

Cooking hacks

Eat more stir-fry: Stir-frying is a quick and easy way to eat vegetables when they are at their nutritional peak. Use a hot pan and, as the name suggests, quickly stir and fry the ingredients for just a couple of minutes to get nutrients and crunch from a variety of vegetables.

Use grains other than white rice: White rice digests very easily, causing a spike in blood sugar that causes a crash of hunger shortly after. Using fibre-rich grains slows the digestion process and gives the meal more nutrition, keeping hunger at bay for longer. Use brown rice instead, or swap in quinoa or mung bean, vegetable or konjac noodles.

Ditch the salt: Use reduced sodium or salt-free seasonings whenever possible and switch to low-sodium or salt-free stocks, broths and bouillons. Sodium contributes to high blood pressure, which is associated with many heart health risks.

Make soup: People from all corners of the earth embrace soup for good reason. Once you get the basic technique, try making your own personal soup recipe that combines some of your favourite flavours. Low-sodium broth, fresh vegetables and grains or beans combine to make a feel-good meal that is satisfying and promotes wellness.

Spice it up: Spices are a great way to add flavour and health benefits to ethnic dishes. Aromatics such as garlic, onion, ginger and chilies have been shown to have beneficial effects on gut health and immunity.

Try plant-based proteins: You don't have to be vegetarian or vegan to appreciate the odd plant-based meal once in a while. Many beans and soy products are rich in polyphenols and fibre, which have great health benefits and are also super-satisfying. Tofu soaks up whatever it is paired with, making it a great carrier for your favourite flavours.

Toast more than your bread: Toasting nuts, dried lentils, grains and spices in a dry pan before cooking increases the flavour.

Use vegetable water: Save some of the water from cooking vegetables, and ladle it in when you are cooking grains such as rice and quinoa. It adds some of the nutrition that has leached out of the vegetables during the boiling process, and often some good flavour too.

Buy marked down items to eat that day: Produce is often marked down in the grocery store when it can't survive a few more days at home, but it is usually perfect for cooking that night or eating for lunch the next day.

Use fresh herbs: Bright, grassy and earthy notes from herbs add a lot of impact both in terms of flavour and visual appeal. Clean and dry fresh herbs before storing them in the fridge; wrap the clean, dry leaves in paper towel to keep leaves from getting damp and prematurely rotting.

Embrace variety: It's great to have a few quick and easy staple meals, but our bodies are designed to eat a blend of foods and balance the goodness from each of them. Try to eat a variety of different healthy foods to ensure your diet is nutritionally balanced.

Buy what's in season: Produce that is in season is not only cheaper, it's usually packed with more flavour and nutrition.

Pack lunches the night before: We all intend to throw together a lunch in the morning, but the morning time crunch inevitably gets in the way. The best (and easiest!) way to pack a lunch is to make more dinner. Pack lunches from your extra cooking before eating that last meal of the day.

Don't expect "restaurant" food: Ethnic food trucks and restaurants prepare foods to appeal to a North American palate, so they're often less spicy, and contain more fat, sugar and salt than the authentic versions. But don't worry, the authentic versions taste great — sometimes even better than the restaurant versions.

Take classes: I know, another class is not something a student wants to think about. But food is a big part of culture, and people love to share their culture — especially if they live in a new country. Visit a supermarket, specialty shop or restaurant to find cooking classes, or even look over someone's shoulder while they cook. Often people are more than happy to share their own tips for cooking some of their favourite dishes.

Tools of the trade

Crockpot/slow cooker: This allows you to have supper ready to eat as you walk in the door after a long day. They come in various sizes, but I would recommend a medium or large one so there's ample room to cook.

Spill-proof glass lunch containers: These can go directly into the microwave or dishwasher without any chemical leaching. They are easy to clean, spill-proof and will last for years.

Vegetable spiralizer: This makes vegetables the vehicle for the good stuff. It also creates a lot of visual appeal for your meal.

Non-stick frying pan: A good quality frying pan makes it easy to prepare foods with a minimal amount of fat.

Oil mister: This is for the times you need some oil, but don't want the dish drenched in it.

Hand/immersion blender: This purées soups and stews without having to transfer to a traditional blender.

Measuring cups, spoons and scale: The human brain has a magnificent way of underestimating quantities of food when measuring by eye. Until you get really savvy in the kitchen and know your own tastes, rely on the accuracy of measuring.

Wok: A stainless steel wok is a great way to make a quick stir-fry for dinner. Woks can go to a much higher heat than is suggested for a non-stick frying pan, allowing you to cook vegetables very quickly and preserve some of their nutrients.

Brekkie

peanut Butter
& Fresh Fruit Waffle Sandwich

INGREDIENTS

- [ ] 2 store-bought whole-grain frozen waffles, toasted
- [ ] 2 tbsp (30 mL) natural peanut butter
- [ ] $^1/_2$ banana, thinly sliced in rounds
- [ ] $^1/_4$ cup (60 mL) berries of your choice, thinly sliced if large
- [ ] $^1/_2$ tbsp (7 mL) liquid honey
- [ ] Pinch cinnamon

Frozen store-bought waffles are rarely thought of as a healthy food, however, there are often whole-grain options available — making them higher in fibre and protein and about half the calories of a bagel. This vegan option is super-healthy and fast for rushed mornings, but eggs, lean sausage and other savoury fillings work really well with a bit more time.

1. Spread top of one waffle with peanut butter.

2. Top with banana and berries. Drizzle with honey and sprinkle with cinnamon.

3. Top with remaining waffle to form sandwich.

Makes 1 serving

TIP:
If using an extra-large whole-grain waffle, just toast it on its own, then fill and fold it in half.

VEGETARIAN

VEGAN

DUTCH

Cheesy Broccoli
FRITTATA

INGREDIENTS

- [ ] 6 eggs
- [ ] 1/4 cup (60 mL) milk
- [ ] 2 tbsp (30 mL) olive oil
- [ ] 1/2 yellow onion, diced
- [ ] 1 cup (250 mL) chopped broccoli
- [ ] Salt and pepper to taste
- [ ] 1/2 cup (125 mL) shredded cheddar cheese

Frittatas are a low-maintenance meal — they are great for using up leftovers, can be eaten anytime, no fussy cooking is involved and there's very little cleanup. You can enjoy frittata between two slices of toast as a breakfast sandwich, crumbled over a salad for extra protein or simply on its own with your favourite condiments.

1. Preheat oven to 425°F (215°C).

2. In bowl, whisk eggs with milk until blended and smooth. Set aside.

3. In ovenproof frying pan over medium-high heat, warm oil. Sauté onion, broccoli, salt and pepper until vegetables are tender, about 5 minutes.

4. Pour egg mixture into pan and sprinkle evenly with cheese.

5. Bake in oven until centre is set, about 10 to 15 minutes.

6. Let cool slightly. Cut into wedges and serve.

Makes 3 to 4 servings

> **VARIATIONS:**
> Try using different combinations of vegetables and cheese such as diced zucchini, black beans and crumbled feta cheese, sliced mushrooms and onion, and shredded Swiss cheese, diced tomato, torn fresh basil and shredded mozzarella cheese

VEGETARIAN

ITALIAN

Spinach, Mushroom
& Feta Omelette

INGREDIENTS

- [ ] Cooking spray, for pan
- [ ] ¹/₂ cup (125 mL) sliced mushrooms (white or cremini)
- [ ] 2 eggs, beaten
- [ ] ¹/₂ cup (125 mL) packed baby spinach
- [ ] ¹/₄ cup (60 mL) crumbled feta cheese
- [ ] Salt and pepper to taste

Earthy mushroom and spinach flavours are balanced by salty feta in this hearty, yet inexpensive, meal. Much healthier than the versions found at greasy spoons, the veggies tucked inside are nutrient rich and this one won't be dripping in oil. Try packing this alongside a piece of fresh fruit to bring brown-bagged lunches back to life, or as an easy and quick backup plan for supper.

1. Warm non-stick pan over medium-high heat, then spritz with cooking spray. Sauté mushrooms until tender, about 4 minutes.

2. Reduce heat to low and pour eggs into pan, gently swirling to coat.

3. Cook, gently lifting edge with spatula, allowing uncooked eggs to run underneath.

4. When eggs are slightly set, arrange spinach and cheese evenly on top and sprinkle with salt and pepper. With spatula, fold in half.

5. Cover and cook until spinach is wilted and eggs are cooked through, 1 to 2 minutes.

Makes 1 serving

VEGETARIAN

GREEK

Tomato, Mozzarella
& Pesto Omelette

INGREDIENTS

- ☐ Cooking spray, for pan
- ☐ 2 eggs
- ☐ 1 tbsp (15 mL) store-bought pesto, divided
- ☐ ¼ cup (60 mL) shredded mozzarella cheese
- ☐ 1 tbsp (15 mL) sliced black olives (optional)
- ☐ ½ tomato, thinly sliced
- ☐ Freshly cracked black pepper

Prepared pesto is a tasty, inexpensive and versatile condiment to keep on hand — try it as a marinade for veggies, mixed with mayo on a sandwich or in this super-easy omelette.

1. In bowl, whisk eggs with about half of the pesto until blended and smooth. Set aside.

2. Warm non-stick frying pan over medium-high heat, then spritz with cooking spray. Reduce heat to low and pour egg mixture into pan, gently swirling to coat.

3. Cook, gently lifting edge with spatula, allowing uncooked egg mixture to run underneath.

4. When egg mixture is slightly set, evenly sprinkle cheese and olives (if using) overtop, then spread tomato slices on one half. With spatula, fold other half overtop.

5. Cook until just warmed through, 1 to 2 minutes. With back of spoon, smear remaining pesto overtop and black pepper to taste.

Makes 1 serving

VEGETARIAN

ITALIAN

Spinach, Tomato
& Herb "coffee cup" Quiche

INGREDIENTS

- ☐ Cooking spray, for mug
- ☐ 1 egg
- ☐ 1¹/₂ tbsp (22 mL) milk
- ☐ 1 tsp (5 mL) canola oil
- ☐ Salt and pepper to taste
- ☐ 3 small grape tomatoes, halved
- ☐ ¹/₄ cup (60 mL) chopped spinach
- ☐ 1 tsp (5 mL) crumbled dried herbs such as minced green onion, parsley or basil

Fast and healthy foods in single-serving sizes couldn't be more fitting for a student's lifestyle. Try this quiche as a quick breakfast, a midnight snack or even when the sink is so full of dishes you can't possibly cook anything else. Try varying the filling to find your perfect quiche!

1. Coat inside of large microwaveable mug with cooking spray.

2. Add egg, milk, oil, salt and pepper; whisk until blended and smooth.

3. Stir in tomatoes, spinach and herbs.

4. Microwave on high until egg mixture is puffed and cooked through, about 1 minute.

Makes 1 serving

VARIATIONS:
Try using different combinations of vegetables, cheese and even leftover meat and grains such as
- Diced ham and green onion, and shredded cheddar cheese
- Diced tomato, shredded mozzarella cheese and fresh basil
- Cooked rice, diced onion and fresh cilantro

VEGETARIAN

NORTH AMERICAN

Zucchini, Cheddar & Basil
"Muffin Tin" Quiche

INGREDIENTS

- [ ] Cooking spray, for pan
- [ ] 8 eggs
- [ ] ¼ cup (60 mL) milk
- [ ] Salt and pepper to taste
- [ ] ¾ cup (175 mL) shredded cheddar cheese
- [ ] 1 medium or 2 small zucchini, diced
- [ ] 1 tbsp (15 mL) olive oil
- [ ] 1 tbsp crumbled dried basil

Breakfast that doesn't require utensils for eating ... light, portable and definitely satisfying. Stash a couple of these in plastic sandwich bags for a protein-rich snack after a workout or to stave off hunger during a long exam. You can also serve them hot — of course — with a green salad on the side or as the filling for a toasted English muffin.

1. Preheat oven to 375°F (190°C).

2. Coat inside of 12-cup muffin tin with cooking spray. Set aside.

3. In bowl, whisk eggs, milk, salt and pepper until blended and smooth; stir in cheese. Set aside.

4. In non-stick frying pan over medium-high heat, toss together zucchini, oil and basil. Sauté until zucchini is tender, about 5 minutes.

5. Evenly divide egg mixture among muffin cups. Evenly spoon zucchini mixture overtop.

6. Bake in oven until egg mixture is puffed and golden, 10 to 15 minutes.

7. Let cool in pan on rack for about 5 minutes before serving.

Makes 6 servings of 2 quiches each

VARIATIONS:
Try using different combinations of vegetables, cheese and even leftover meat and grains such as
- Salsa, black beans and shredded cheddar cheese
- Diced ham, spinach and crumbled feta cheese
- Diced tomatos and olives, and fresh dill

VEGETARIAN

NORTH AMERICAN

Prep: 5 min | Cook: 15 min

White Bean
SHAKSHUKA

INGREDIENTS

- [ ] 1 tbsp (15 mL) olive oil
- [ ] 2 small onions, diced
- [ ] 4 cloves garlic, minced
- [ ] 1 tsp (5 mL) crumbled dried sage
- [ ] 1/2 tsp (2 mL) red pepper flakes
- [ ] 2 tbsp (30 mL) liquid honey or packed brown sugar
- [ ] 2 tbsp (30 mL) ketchup
- [ ] 1 can (19 oz/650 mL) tomato sauce
- [ ] 1 can (14 oz/398 mL) white beans, drained and rinsed
- [ ] 2 tbsp (30 mL) balsamic vinegar
- [ ] Salt and pepper to taste
- [ ] 4 eggs
- [ ] Sprigs of parsley and/or pats of butter, for garnish (optional)

VEGETARIAN

MIDDLE EASTERN

Cook this spicy and warm Israeli dish once, then eat multiple times for less than a dollar per serving! Beans are not only inexpensive, they're a great source of fibre and protein — nutrients that promote a speedy metabolism. Enjoy this dish any time of day, with some veggies on the side to make it a balanced meal.

1. In large Dutch oven or cast-iron pan over medium-high heat, warm oil. Sauté onions, scraping up brown bits from bottom of pan, until tender and golden.

2. Stir in garlic, sage and red pepper flakes. Sauté for about 2 minutes.

3. Stir in honey and ketchup until paste forms.

4. Stir in tomato sauce. Reduce heat and bring to a gentle simmer.

5. Stir in beans, vinegar, salt and pepper.

6. Working around edge of pan, add eggs, one at a time, as follows: push bowl of ladle down into mixture, creating space for one egg; crack egg into small cup, then pour into space.

7. Cook until eggs are preferred doneness, 3 to 5 minutes.

8. Divide into 4 servings with 1 egg in each. Garnish with parsley and/or butter.

Makes 4 servings

TIP:
Cracking eggs into a small bowl or mug instead of directly into a hot pan allows you to check for eggshells before they're added to the dish.

scrambled Egg
& Black Bean Burritos

INGREDIENTS

- ☐ 1 tbsp (15 mL) olive oil
- ☐ 2 cloves garlic, minced or pressed
- ☐ 1 can (14 oz/398 mL) black beans, drained and rinsed
- ☐ 4 eggs
- ☐ 2 tbsp (30 mL) milk
- ☐ 1/4 cup (60 mL) chopped fresh cilantro leaves (optional)
- ☐ 4 small flour tortillas, warmed (see TIP below)
- ☐ 1/2 cup (125 mL) store-bought salsa
- ☐ 1/4 cup (60 mL) shredded cheddar or Monterey Jack cheese

Breakfast burritos are warm, satisfying and portable. This recipe is a classic — and hard to beat — but feel free to add other vegetables or proteins to your burritos, to use up leftovers or just to try something new.

1. In non-stick pan over medium heat, warm oil. Sauté garlic for about 2 minutes or until the golden and fragrant.

2. Increase heat to medium-high and add beans. Sauté until warmed through, about 5 minutes.

3. In bowl, whisk eggs with milk until blended and smooth. Stir into pan.

4. Stir with spatula until cooked through. Remove from heat and stir in cilantro (if using).

5. Lay tortillas flat on work surface. Top each with one-quarter of the egg and bean mixture, salsa and cheese. Roll up to form burritos.

Makes 4 burritos

VEGETARIAN

TEX-MEX

! TIP:
Cover and microwave tortillas on high until warmed through, about 1 minute.

Salmon, Cream Cheese
& Cucumber Bagel

INGREDIENTS

- ☐ 1 whole-grain bagel, halved and toasted
- ☐ 2 tbsp (30 mL) cream cheese
- ☐ 2 oz (55 g) smoked salmon
- ☐ 4 to 6 slices English cucumber
- ☐ 1/2 tbsp (7 mL) diced red onion
- ☐ 1/2 tbsp (7 mL) capers (optional)

This simple sandwich that most people associate with afternoon tea makes a great portable breakfast or a quick and easy supper. Bonus points for the heart-healthy fat in salmon that benefits brain function. Try this out as a meatless Monday option that doesn't sacrifice flavour or protein.

1. Spread each cut edge of bagel with half of the cheese. Arrange half each of the salmon, cucumber, onion and capers (if using) overtop.

Makes 1 serving

TIP:
If you're in a hurry, just pile all of the ingredients on the bottom of the bagel, sandwich with the top and enjoy!

EASTERN EUROPEAN

Avocado Toast:
10 WAYS

INGREDIENTS

- [ ] ½ avocado, diced
- [ ] Salt and pepper to taste
- [ ] Suggested flavour combination, below
- [ ] 1 slice bread, toasted

When life is crazy and hectic, and a million assignments are due at once, avocado toast in all its simplicity will never disappoint. Hearty bread, such as sourdough, pumpernickel or whole-grain, makes the creaminess of the avocado stand out that much more. Try any of these interesting flavour profiles or create your own. It's impossible to go wrong.

1. In small bowl with fork, mash together avocado, salt and pepper until evenly mixed.

2. Spread avocado over toast and layer chosen flavor combination on top.

Makes 1 serving

FLAVOUR COMBINATIONS:
- Sliced tomato and red onion
- Poached egg and store-bought tomato bruschetta
- Fresh cilantro and lime juice
- Pineapple slices and red pepper flakes
- Sliced mango and curry powder
- Sliced cucumber and radish, and fresh dill
- Sliced strawberries, balsamic vinegar and fresh mint
- Store-bought hot sauce and lemon juice
- Crumbled feta cheese and diced green onion
- Goat cheese and drizzled liquid honey

VEGAN

VEGETARIAN

AUSTRALIAN

Rolled Oat Pancakes
& Simple Ginger Blueberry Sauce

INGREDIENTS

- [ ] 1 soft ripe banana
- [ ] 1 tsp (5 mL) baking powder
- [ ] 1 egg or 'flax egg" (see VARIATION below)
- [ ] 1/4 cup (60 mL) milk or milk alternative
- [ ] 1/2 tsp (2 mL) vanilla extract
- [ ] 1/4 cup (60 mL) whole wheat flour
- [ ] 3/4 cup (125 mL) rolled oats
- [ ] 1/2 tsp (2 mL) cinnamon
- [ ] Pinch of salt
- [ ] Cooking spray, for pan

SAUCE

- [ ] 1 tbsp (15 mL) coconut oil
- [ ] 1/2 tsp (2 mL) ground ginger
- [ ] 1/2 cup (125 mL) blueberries (fresh or frozen)
- [ ] 1/4 cup (60 mL) liquid honey, agave syrup or maple syrup

Rolled oats are incredibly heart-healthy and inexpensive; it only makes sense to repurpose them in ways other than the typical hot cereal. These 'oatmeal" pancakes are wholesome, nutrient rich and filling. Try topping these with additional fruit or bump up the protein with a dollop of yogurt or natural nut butter.

1. Sauce: In small saucepan over medium heat, melt coconut oil. Sauté ginger for about 30 seconds.

2. Stir in blueberries and honey. Reduce heat to low, cover and keep warm.

3. In bowl with fork, mash banana with baking powder until smooth.

4. Stir in egg, milk and vanilla until blended and smooth.

5. Stir in flour until blended and smooth; stir in oats, cinnamon and salt to combine.

6. Warm non-stick frying pan over medium-high heat. Coat with cooking spray.

7. One at a time, cook pancakes. Pour one-quarter of the banana mixture into pan, gently swirling to coat; cook, without stirring, until golden brown on bottom, 2 to 4 minutes.

8. Gently turn over. Cook until golden brown on bottom and cooked through, 2 to 4 minutes. Serve with sauce.

Makes 4 small or 2 large pancakes

VARIATION:
1. Make this recipe vegan by using the flax egg and a milk alternative such as soy or almond.
2. Try using different fruits in the simple sauce: strawberry, mango and peach all pair excellently with ginger.

MAKE AHEAD:
Allow cooked pancakes to cool at room temperature and wrap securely in plastic wrap to freeze for a later time. Unwrap and microwave for 30 seconds to 1 minute to reheat from frozen.

VEGETARIAN

VEGAN

SCOTTISH

BANANA PANCAKES

INGREDIENTS

- [ ] 2 eggs
- [ ] 1 soft ripe banana
- [ ] $1/2$ cup (125 mL) raspberries (optional)
- [ ] Maple syrup, liquid honey or agave syrup

Flourless and with simple ingredients, this whole–food–based pancake recipe is a cinch. This is a great breakfast to double- or triple-batch cook, so you can freeze the extras, then microwave for just a few seconds to reheat as a quick morning meal or snack. Sandwiching a spoonful of peanut butter or a handful of chocolate chips between two pancakes is great, but both together are blissful.

1. In blender, purée eggs with banana until blended and smooth.

2. Heat non-stick frying pan over medium-high heat.

3. One at a time, cook pancakes. Pour half of the egg mixture into pan, gently swirling to coat. Cook, without stirring, until bubbles begin forming on top, about 1 minute.

4. Gently turn over. Cook until golden colour develops, about 1 minute more.

5. Transfer to serving plates. Divide raspberries evenly on top (if using). Serve with your favourite syrup.

Makes 2 servings

> **VARIATION:**
> Blend in pinch of cinnamon or $1/2$ tsp (2 mL) vanilla or almond extract.

VEGETARIAN

ASIAN (THAI)

Apple Berry
BREAKFAST CRISP

INGREDIENTS

- [ ] Cooking spray, for baking dish
- [ ] 4 unpeeled Granny Smith apples, quartered, cored and diced
- [ ] 2 cups (500 mL) any combination of berries
- [ ] ¹/₄ cup (60 mL) packed brown sugar
- [ ] 2 tbsp (30 mL) whole wheat flour
- [ ] 1 tbsp (15 mL) lemon juice
- [ ] 2 tsp (10 mL) cinnamon

TOPPING

- [ ] ³/₄ cup (175 mL) rolled oats
- [ ] ¹/₄ cup (60 mL) packed brown sugar
- [ ] 4 tbsp (75 mL) butter, softened
- [ ] 4 tbsp (75 mL) walnut pieces (optional)
- [ ] 2 tbsp (30 mL) whole wheat flour

Crisp isn't just for dessert — reduced sugar and increased fruit make this version a delicious and balanced morning meal. Try serving this crisp topped with a generous dollop of Greek yogurt or some extra nuts for protein.

1. Preheat the oven to 350°F (180°C).

2. Coat glass or ceramic baking dish with cooking spray.

3. In bowl, toss together apples, berries, brown sugar, flour, lemon juice and cinnamon to coat. Scrape into prepared baking dish.

4. Topping: In bowl with fork, stir together oats, brown sugar, butter, walnuts (if using) and flour until in large crumbs. Sprinkle evenly over apple mixture.

5. Bake in oven until apples are tender and topping is golden and crisp, 30 to 35 minutes.

Makes 6 servings

VEGETARIAN

VEGAN

ENGLISH

TIP:
Convert this crisp to a vegan version by using vegan butter or solid coconut oil.

MAKE AHEAD:
Let cool. Cover with plastic wrap and refrigerate for up to 4 days.

Applesauce French Toast
Casserole

INGREDIENTS

- ☐ Cooking spray, for baking dish
- ☐ 3 1/2 cups (875 mL) cubed bread
- ☐ 1 1/2 cups (375 mL) milk
- ☐ 1 cup (250 mL) silken tofu or yogurt
- ☐ 1/2 cup (125 mL) applesauce
- ☐ 3 tbsp (45 mL) maple syrup
- ☐ 2 tsp (10 mL) vanilla extract
- ☐ 1/2 tsp (2 mL) nutmeg
- ☐ 2 tsp (10 mL) cinnamon, divided
- ☐ 1/4 cup (60 mL) packed brown sugar
- ☐ 2 tbsp (30 mL) raisins

French toast is a fantastic way to use up stale bread. Try topping this recipe with some fresh fruit and cottage cheese, then serve with a side of breakfast ham to make a luscious brunch.

1. Preheat the oven to 400°F (200°C).

2. Coat small to medium glass or ceramic baking dish with cooking spray. Arrange bread cubes evenly over bottom, gently pressing flat.

3. In blender, purée milk, tofu, applesauce, maple syrup, vanilla, nutmeg and half of the cinnamon until blended and smooth. Pour evenly over bread.

4. Cover with plastic wrap. Refrigerate overnight.

5. In bowl with fork, stir together brown sugar, raisins and remaining cinnamon. Sprinkle over milk mixture in pan.

6. Bake in oven until set, 30 to 35 minutes.

Makes 6 servings

TIP:
To make this recipe vegan, use vegan bread and replace dairy milk with soy, almond or coconut milk.

VARIATION:
Substitute canned pumpkin or butternut squash purée for the applesauce.

VEGETARIAN

VEGAN

NORTH AMERICAN

french Toast with
STRAWBERRY SAUCE & HAZELNUTS

INGREDIENTS

- [ ] Cooking spray
- [ ] 1 1/2 cups (375 mL) milk or milk alternative
- [ ] 2 large eggs, beaten
- [ ] 2 tbsp (30 mL) sugar
- [ ] 2 tsp (10 mL) vanilla extract
- [ ] 2 tsp (10 mL) cinnamon
- [ ] 1/2 tsp (3 mL) nutmeg
- [ ] 4 thick slices of white bread
- [ ] 2 cups (500 mL) hulled strawberries, quartered
- [ ] 1/4 cup (60 mL) sugar
- [ ] 1/4 cup (60 mL) cold water
- [ ] 2 tsp (10 mL) cornstarch
- [ ] 1/2 cup (125 mL) flaked hazelnuts/filberts

1. Coat a non-stick pan with cooking spray and place over medium heat. Place a parchment-lined baking sheet in the oven at 200°F (90°C).

2. In a large mixing bowl, whisk together the milk, eggs, sugar, vanilla, cinnamon and nutmeg.

3. Dunk a slice of bread in the milk mixture and place in the hot pan. Repeat for a second slice of bread if space in the pan allows.

4. Cook until the underside of the bread is golden, about 3 minutes, and carefully flip over. Transfer the cooked piece of French toast to the pan in the oven to keep warm.

5. While cooking the French toast, place a medium saucepan over medium heat. Add the strawberries, sugar, water and cornstarch.

6. Stir until smooth and cover to cook and thicken for about 5 to 10 minutes.

7. In a dry frying pan over medium-low heat, gently warm the flaked hazelnuts to gently toast them, tossing constantly. Be careful not to burn, as they will toast very quickly.

8. Drizzle bread with strawberry sauce and a tablespoon of toasted hazelnuts.

Makes 4 servings

VEGETARIAN

ENGLISH

Chipotle
Sweet Potato Soup

INGREDIENTS

- [ ] 1 tbsp (15 mL) canola oil
- [ ] 1 yellow onion, diced
- [ ] 1 tbsp (15 mL) chipotle paste
- [ ] 1/2 tsp (2 mL) cinnamon
- [ ] Salt and pepper to taste
- [ ] 4 cups (1 L) vegetable stock
- [ ] 2 large sweet potatoes, grated
- [ ] 1/4 cup (60 mL) fresh cilantro leaves

This super-simple vegan soup is crammed with nutrition and smoky chipotle flavour. Add a few crumbles of salty feta on top or a dollop of good-quality sour cream to make it extra decadent.

1. In large heavy-bottomed saucepan over medium-high heat, warm oil. Sauté onion until tender and fragrant.

2. Stir in chipotle paste, cinnamon, salt and pepper. Sauté for about 1 minute.

3. Stir in vegetable stock and sweet potatoes. Reduce heat, cover and simmer until potatoes are tender, 10 to 15 minutes.

4. Transfer to blender. Purée until blended and smooth (see TIP below).

5. Return to pan over medium heat; cook, stirring, until heated through. Garnish each serving with cilantro leaves.

Makes 4 servings

> **TIP:**
> You can use an immersion blender to purée soup while it's still in the pot. If you are using a stand blender, let soup cool slightly before ladling it into the blender, to avoid spills and burns, and also to prevent pressure from steam from popping the lid off the blender.

VEGETARIAN

VEGAN

TEX-MEX

Coconut Carrot
& Chili Soup

INGREDIENTS

- [ ] ¹/₄ cup (60 mL) coconut oil
- [ ] 2 cloves garlic, crushed
- [ ] 1 yellow onion, diced
- [ ] 1 lb (450 g) carrots, chopped small
- [ ] 2 cups (500 mL) low-sodium chicken or vegetable stock
- [ ] 1 can (14 oz/398 mL) coconut milk
- [ ] 2 tbsp (30 mL) Thai sweet chili sauce
- [ ] Salt and pepper to taste
- [ ] Fresh cilantro leaves, thinly sliced green onion and/or peanut pieces to garnish

Served hot or cold, this creamy, sweet and spicy dish is great for using up that bag of carrots you thought would never empty. It also tastes so good that you'll probably never believe that it's healthy! Its immunity-boosting healthy fats, spices and vitamin A make freezing a portion for the next time you're feeling under the weather a really good idea.

1. In large, heavy-bottomed saucepan over medium-high heat, melt coconut oil. Sauté garlic and onion until tender and fragrant.

2. Stir in carrots and chicken stock. Cook, scraping up brown bits from bottom of pan (see TIPS below).

3. Reduce heat and simmer until carrots are tender, about 15 to 20 minutes.

4. Stir in coconut milk and chili sauce. Cook for 5 minutes.

5. Purée until blended and smooth (see TIPS below).

6. Return to pan over medium heat. Cook, stirring, until heated through.

7. Garnish each serving with cilantro leaves, green onion and/or peanut pieces.

Makes 4 servings

VEGETARIAN

VEGAN

ASIAN (THAI)

> **TIPS:**
> Scraping up brown bits from the bottom of the pan is a process called "deglazing" that adds depth of flavour to the dish.
> You can use an immersion blender to purée soup while it's still in the pot. If you are using a stand blender, let soup cool slightly before ladling it into the blender, to avoid spills and burns, and also to prevent pressure from steam from popping the lid off the blender.

Butternut squash
& Apple Soup

INGREDIENTS

- [ ] 2 tbsp (30 mL) butter
- [ ] 1 onion, diced
- [ ] 1-inch (2.5 cm) piece fresh ginger, minced
- [ ] 1 tbsp (15 mL) curry powder
- [ ] 2 Granny Smith apples, cored and cubed
- [ ] 1 large potato, cubed
- [ ] 2 cups (500 mL) cubed butternut squash
- [ ] 1 cup (250 mL) carrot rounds
- [ ] 4 cups (1 L) chicken stock
- [ ] 1 cup (250 mL) milk (or ½ cup/125 mL cream)
- [ ] Salt and pepper to taste
- [ ] ¼ cup (60 mL) green onion, thinly sliced on diagonal

SOUTH AFRICAN

Tart apples and sweet, earthy squash — the best of fall flavours come together in this hearty meal. I suggest topping it with a few crispy, smoky bacon bits if you're feeling self-indulgent.

1. In large stockpot over medium-high heat, melt butter. Sauté onion and ginger until softened and beginning to brown.

2. Stir in curry powder and cook for 1 minute. Toss in apples, potato, squash and carrots to coat.

3. Stir in chicken stock. Reduce heat and simmer until potatoes are tender, about 10 minutes.

4. Purée until blended and smooth (see TIP below). Return to pan over medium heat. Stir in milk, salt and pepper and cook, stirring, until heated through.

5. Garnish each serving with green onions.

Makes 6 servings

> **!**
> **TIP:**
> You can use an immersion blender to purée soup while it's still in the pot. If you are using a stand blender, let soup cool slightly before ladling it into the blender, to avoid spills and burns, and also to prevent pressure from steam from popping the lid off the blender.

Hot & spicy
Tomato Soup

INGREDIENTS

- [ ] 2 tbsp (30 mL) olive oil
- [ ] 2 cloves garlic, minced
- [ ] 1 yellow onion, diced
- [ ] 1 carrot, diced
- [ ] 1 stalk celery, diced
- [ ] 1 tsp (5 mL) red pepper flakes
- [ ] 1 can (28 oz / 796 mL) diced tomatoes, with juice
- [ ] 2 cups (500 mL) vegetable stock
- [ ] 1 tbsp (30 mL) tomato paste
- [ ] 2 tbsp (30 mL) packed brown sugar
- [ ] Salt and pepper to taste
- [ ] 1 cup (250 mL) milk

A childhood favourite taken up a notch, spicy tomato soup is miles ahead of the canned stuff. This soup makes a fantastic meal with a grilled cheese sandwich on the side, but is equally satisfying on its own. Immunity-boosting spice and vitamin C from the tomatoes and onion make this a great staple for warding off a nagging cold during the school year.

1. In large saucepan over medium-high heat, warm oil and sauté garlic, onion, carrot, celery and red pepper flakes, stirring occasionally, until vegetables are tender, about 10 minutes.

2. Stir in tomatoes, vegetable stock, tomato paste, brown sugar, salt and pepper. Simmer, stirring occasionally, for 20 minutes.

3. Purée until blended and smooth (see TIP below).

4. Return to pan over medium heat. Stir in milk and cook, stirring, until heated through.

Makes 4 to 6 servings

TIP:
You can use an immersion blender to purée soup while it's still in the pot. If you are using a stand blender, let soup cool slightly before ladling it into the blender, to avoid spills and burns, and also to prevent pressure from steam from popping the lid off the blender.

MAKE AHEAD:
Combine raw ingredients in resealable freezer bag, seal and "massage" lightly to coat vegetables; freeze for a slow cooker meal. Alternatively, transfer single-serving portions of finished soup to airtight containers and freeze for quick microwaveable meals.

VEGETARIAN

SPANISH

Black Bean
& Tortilla Soup

INGREDIENTS

- [ ] 2 tbsp (30 mL) olive oil
- [ ] 4 cloves garlic, minced
- [ ] 1 yellow onion, diced
- [ ] 1 carrot, chopped
- [ ] 1 jalapeño pepper, diced
- [ ] 2 tsp (10 mL) ground cumin
- [ ] 2 cans (each 19 oz/540 mL) black beans, drained and rinsed
- [ ] 1 can (28 oz/796 mL) diced tomatoes, with juice
- [ ] 2 cups (500 mL) vegetable stock
- [ ] 1 avocado, cubed
- [ ] 1/4 cup (60 mL) lime juice
- [ ] Salt and pepper to taste
- [ ] 1 or 2 handfuls low-sodium whole-grain tortilla chips, broken

This vegan soup is thick and hearty, simple to make and super-easy on the budget. It's so zippy and flavourful, no one will believe it's good for you, too.

1. In large stockpot over medium-high heat, warm oil. Sauté garlic, onion and carrot until tender, about 4 minutes.

2. Stir in jalapeño and cumin. Sauté for about 2 minutes.

3. Stir in beans, tomatoes and vegetable stock until combined.

4. Immediately transfer 2 cups (500 mL) to blender. Purée until blended and smooth, then return to pot. (Alternatively, use an immersion blender and pulse directly in the pot to partially purée the soup.)

5. Cook, stirring occasionally, until heated through, about 10 minutes.

6. In small, non-reactive bowl, toss together avocado, lime juice, salt and pepper to coat (see TIP below).

7. Divide soup evenly among 6 serving bowls; top with tortilla chips and scoop of avocado mixture.

Makes 6 servings

TIP:
The vitamin C in juice from citrus fruits — such as lemons, limes and oranges — prevents fresh-cut fruits and veggies from oxidizing and turning brown. The juice also tastes really good!

VEGETARIAN

VEGAN

MEXICAN

Minted pea soup

INGREDIENTS

- [ ] 1 tbsp (15 mL) canola oil
- [ ] 1 white potato, grated
- [ ] 1/2 yellow onion, grated
- [ ] 1 clove garlic, crushed
- [ ] 4 cups (1 L) low-sodium vegetable or chicken stock
- [ ] 1 cup (250 mL) frozen peas
- [ ] 1/4 cup (60 mL) packed fresh mint leaves, chopped
- [ ] 1 tbsp (15 mL) lemon juice
- [ ] 1/2 tbsp (7 mL) sugar
- [ ] 2/3 cup (150 mL) Greek yogurt
- [ ] Salt and pepper to taste

Delicious both hot and cold, this soup is great as a starter or as a side.

1. In large, heavy-bottomed saucepan over medium-high heat, warm oil; sauté potato and onion until onion is softened. Stir in garlic; sauté for about 1 minute. Stir in vegetable stock, increase heat to high and bring to a simmer; reduce heat, cover and simmer until potato is tender, about 5 minutes. Stir in peas, mint, lemon juice and sugar.

2. Transfer to blender and purée until blended and smooth (or see TIP below). Return to pan over medium heat.

3. Stir in yogurt, salt and pepper; cook, stirring, until heated through.

Makes 4 servings

TIP:
You can use an immersion blender to purée soup while it's still in the pot. If you are using a stand blender, let soup cool slightly before ladling it into the blender to avoid spills and burns, and also to prevent pressure from steam from popping the lid off the blender.

VEGETARIAN

ENGLISH

loaded Baked
Potato Chowder

INGREDIENTS

- [ ] 6 slices bacon, diced (about 12 oz/340 g)
- [ ] 6 cloves garlic, minced
- [ ] 1 white onion, diced
- [ ] 3 tbsp (45 mL) all-purpose flour
- [ ] 3 cups (750 mL) low-sodium chicken stock
- [ ] 2 cups (500 mL) milk
- [ ] 4 cups (1 L) diced unpeeled potatoes (about 1 1/2 lb/675 g)
- [ ] 1 jalapeño pepper, seeded and diced or 1 can (4 oz/114 mL) chopped green chilies
- [ ] 1 tbsp (30 mL) Old Bay Seasoning
- [ ] 1/2 tsp (2 mL) crumbled dried thyme or savory
- [ ] 1 can (14 oz/398 mL) corn kernels, drained
- [ ] 1 cup (250 mL) shredded old cheddar cheese
- [ ] 1/4 tsp (2 mL) cayenne pepper
- [ ] 2 green onions, thinly sliced on diagonal

Brimming with smoky, sweet and earthy flavours, this is a comforting classic made from pantry basics. The velvety mouth feel contrasts perfectly with crusty whole-grain bread.

1. In large stockpot over medium-high heat, sauté bacon until crisp.

2. With slotted spoon, transfer to paper towel to drain.

3. Discard all but 1 tbsp (15 mL) fat from pan. Sauté garlic and onion until softened and golden.

4. Sprinkle flour into pan. Cook, stirring, until combined with fat into paste, 1 to 2 minutes.

5. Stir in chicken stock and milk until blended with paste.

6. Stir in potatoes, jalapeño, Old Bay Seasoning and thyme. Reduce heat, cover and simmer until potatoes are tender, about 15 minutes.

7. Return three-quarters of the bacon to pot. Stir in corn, cheese and cayenne until cheese has melted.

8. Garnish each serving with remaining bacon and green onion.

Makes 6 to 8 servings

ATLANTIC CANADIAN

Chicken Quinoa Soup

INGREDIENTS

- [ ] 2 tbsp (30 mL) olive oil
- [ ] 4 boneless, skinless chicken thighs, cubed
- [ ] 4 cloves garlic, minced
- [ ] 1 yellow onion, diced
- [ ] 1 tbsp (15 mL) crumbled dried thyme or savory
- [ ] 1 carrot, diced
- [ ] 1 stalk celery, diced
- [ ] 6 cups (1.5 L) low-sodium chicken stock
- [ ] 1 sweet potato, diced
- [ ] 4 stalks kale, ribs removed, chopped
- [ ] 1 cup (250 mL) uncooked quinoa
- [ ] ¹/₂ cup (125 mL) frozen peas
- [ ] 1 tbsp (15 mL) lemon juice
- [ ] Salt and pepper to taste

A comfort food in many cultures, chicken soup cures whatever ails you — from headaches to heartbreak. Parents everywhere agree that it's a good idea to freeze and save a portion of this soup to warm up when the next life hurdle strikes.

1. In large stockpot over medium-high heat, warm oil. Sauté chicken, garlic, onion and thyme until cooked through, about 5 to 6 minutes.

2. Stir in carrot and celery. Sauté for 1 to 2 minutes.

3. Stir in chicken stock, scraping up brown bits from bottom of pan.

4. Stir in sweet potato, kale and quinoa. Increase heat to high, cover and boil for 2 to 3 minutes.

5. Reduce heat and simmer, covered, until quinoa is tender and grains are edged with white, 15 to 20 minutes.

6. Stir in peas, lemon juice, salt and pepper.

Makes 8 servings

NORTH AMERICAN

Creamy Tomato, Basil
& Tortellini Soup

INGREDIENTS

- [ ] 2 tbsp (30 mL) olive oil
- [ ] 4 cloves garlic, minced
- [ ] 1 yellow onion, diced
- [ ] 1 carrot, chopped
- [ ] 2 dried bay leaves
- [ ] 1 tbsp (15 mL) dried basil
- [ ] 2 cans (each 28 oz/796 mL) tomatoes, with juice
- [ ] 1 carton (32 oz/750 mL) vegetable stock
- [ ] 2 tbsp (30 mL) packed brown sugar
- [ ] Salt and pepper to taste
- [ ] 2 cups (500 mL) milk
- [ ] 1 lb (450 g) tortellini, cooked
- [ ] ¼ cup (60 mL) grated Parmesan cheese

VEGETARIAN

ITALIAN

Velvety smooth tomatoes and substantial tortellini (stuffed pasta) are a match made in heaven. Try simmering this soup in a slow cooker for about four hours, stir in the cooked tortellini at the end and garnish with Parmesan.

1. In large stockpot over medium-high heat, warm oil. Sauté garlic, onion and carrot until softened.

2. Stir in bay leaves and basil. Sauté for about 1 minute.

3. Stir in tomatoes, vegetable stock, brown sugar, salt and pepper.

4. Reduce heat and simmer, stirring occasionally, for about 10 minutes. Remove and discard bay leaves.

5. Transfer to blender, purée until blended and smooth (or see TIP below). Return to pot over medium heat.

6. Stir in milk until blended and smooth; stir in tortellini. Stir in half of the cheese until melted.

7. Garnish with remaining cheese.

Makes 8 servings

> **TIP:**
> You can use an immersion blender to purée soup while it's still in the pot. If you are using a stand blender, let soup cool slightly before ladling it into the blender, to avoid spills and burns, and also to prevent pressure from steam from popping the lid off the blender.

roasted red pepper soup

INGREDIENTS

- [ ] 2 tbsp (30 mL) olive oil
- [ ] 2 cloves garlic, minced
- [ ] 1 yellow onion, diced
- [ ] 1 carrot, diced
- [ ] 1 stalk celery, diced
- [ ] 1 medium Yukon Gold or Russet potato, diced
- [ ] 1/2 tsp (2 mL) red pepper flakes
- [ ] 1 bay leaf
- [ ] 4 store-bought roasted red peppers
- [ ] 3 cups (750 mL) vegetable stock
- [ ] 1 tbsp (15 mL) packed brown sugar
- [ ] 1 tbsp (15 mL) tomato paste
- [ ] 1/2 cup (125 mL) Greek yogurt (optional)
- [ ] Salt and pepper to taste

Store-bought jars of roasted red peppers are an inexpensive alternative to the fresh versions. This vegan soup is easily made creamy by stirring in some healthy and tangy Greek yogurt instead of traditional cream.

1. In large saucepan over medium-high heat, warm oil. Sauté garlic, onion, carrot, celery, potato, red pepper flakes and bay leaf for 5 minutes or until vegetables are tender.

2. Stir in red peppers, vegetable stock, brown sugar and tomato paste. Simmer, stirring occasionally, for 5 to 10 minutes. Remove and discard bay leaf.

3. Transfer to blender, purée until blended and smooth (or see TIP below). Return to pan over medium heat. Stir in yogurt (if using), salt and pepper until blended and smooth.

Makes 4 servings

TIP:
You can use an immersion blender to purée soup while it's still in the pot. If you are using a stand blender, let soup cool slightly before ladling it into the blender, to avoid spills and burns, and also to prevent pressure from steam from popping the lid off the blender.

MAKE AHEAD:
Combine ingredients in resealable freezer bag, seal and 'massage" lightly to coat vegetables; freeze for a slow cooker meal. Alternatively, transfer single-serving portions of soup to airtight containers and freeze for quick microwaveable meals.

VEGETARIAN

VEGAN

GREEK

rustic Minestrone

VEGETARIAN

VEGAN

ITALIAN

INGREDIENTS

- [ ] 2 tbsp (30 mL) olive oil
- [ ] 6 cloves garlic, minced
- [ ] 1 yellow onion, diced
- [ ] 1 carrot, diced
- [ ] 1 stalk celery, diced
- [ ] 4 stalks kale, ribs removed
- [ ] 2 sweet potatoes, diced
- [ ] 2 zucchini, diced
- [ ] $1/2$ tsp (2 mL) red pepper flakes
- [ ] 1 can (28 oz/796 mL) diced tomatoes, with juice
- [ ] 1 can (19 oz/540 mL) kidney beans, drained and rinsed
- [ ] 4 cups (1 L) vegetable stock
- [ ] $1/2$ cup (125 mL) chopped frozen green beans
- [ ] 1 tbsp (15 mL) lemon juice
- [ ] Salt and pepper to taste
- [ ] 2 tbsp (30 mL) nutritional yeast or grated Parmesan cheese

Chunky vegetables, beans and spice make this soup nothing short of a detox for your body. Try this soup alongside your favourite sandwich, such as the Pesto Tuna & Roasted Red Pepper Sandwich (page 66), for a fulfilling feast.

1. In large stockpot over medium-high heat, warm oil. Sauté garlic and onion until softened.

2. Stir in carrot and celery. Sauté for 1 to 2 minutes.

3. Toss in kale, sweet potatoes, zucchini and red pepper flakes to coat.

4. Stir in tomatoes, beans, vegetable stock. Reduce heat and simmer until vegetables are tender, 10 to 15 minutes.

5. Stir in green beans, lemon juice, salt and pepper.

6. Garnish each serving with generous sprinkle of yeast or Parmesan cheese.

Makes 8 servings

> **TIP:**
> Nutritional yeast is a great pantry staple to have — its large flakes are packed with B vitamins and it has a wonderfully cheesy flavour even though it's vegan friendly. It makes a great addition to salad dressings, soups and sprinkled on pasta.

smoky pumpkin
& White Bean Soup

INGREDIENTS

- [ ] 2 slices bacon, chopped
- [ ] 5 cloves garlic, crushed
- [ ] 1 cup (250 mL) chopped onion
- [ ] 2 tbsp (30 mL) minced fresh sage
- [ ] 1 tsp (5 mL) dried savory
- [ ] 1/4 tsp (2 mL) ground cumin
- [ ] 3 1/2 cups (875 mL) chicken stock
- [ ] 1 cup (250 mL) white beans such as cannellini
- [ ] 1 can (19 oz/540 mL) pumpkin purée
- [ ] 1 cup (250 mL) milk
- [ ] 1 tsp (5 mL) salt
- [ ] 2 tbsp (30 mL) apple cider vinegar

Pumpkin purée is a component we rarely think of as part of a savoury dish, but its creamy texture and healthful nature make it an ingredient to get comfortable with. Try pairing this soup with an Apple, Bacon & Gouda Grilled Cheese (page 71) for a complete meal, or just tote it in a Thermos for a long day at the library

1. In large stockpot over medium-high heat, sauté bacon until crisp.

2. With slotted spoon, transfer to paper towel to drain.

3. Add garlic, onion, sage, savory and cumin to fat in pan. Sauté until tender and beginning to brown.

4. Stir in 1/2 cup (125 mL) of the chicken stock, scraping up any brown bits from bottom of pan.

5. Stir in remaining stock, beans, pumpkin, milk and salt until blended and smooth. Cook for another 5 to 10 minutes for the flavours to develop.

6. Stir in cider vinegar.

7. Garnish with bacon.

Makes 6 servings

VARIATION:

Make this dish vegan by replacing the bacon with 2 tbsp (30 mL) olive oil and the chicken stock with vegetable stock, then garnishing with toasted pine nuts. Sprinkle 1 teaspoon (5 mL) smoked paprika to cooking vegetables in the pan, to ramp up the smoky flavour without adding meat.

VEGETARIAN

VEGAN

HAITIAN

Mushroom
& BARLEY BISQUE

INGREDIENTS

- [ ] 2 tbsp (30 mL) olive oil
- [ ] 8 oz (225 g) sliced cremini or mini-bella mushrooms
- [ ] 4 cloves garlic, minced
- [ ] 1 yellow onion, diced
- [ ] 1 stalk celery, diced
- [ ] 1 tbsp (15 mL) crumbled dried thyme or savory
- [ ] 6 cups (1.5 L) low-sodium chicken stock
- [ ] 2 tbsp (30 mL) soy sauce
- [ ] 1 cup (250 mL) pot or pearl barley, cooked
- [ ] $1/2$ cup (125 mL) chopped parsley
- [ ] $1/2$ cup (125 mL) non-fat yogurt
- [ ] Salt and pepper to taste
- [ ] $1/2$ tbsp (30 mL) butter, cut in 4 pats

Creamy yogurt makes this soup tangy and rich without extra fat from cream. Vary the mushrooms with whatever variety is on sale. This recipe is a perfect side for a slow cooker meat dish.

1. In large stockpot over medium-high heat, warm oil. Sauté mushrooms until deep brown, about 4 to 5 minutes.

2. Stir in garlic, onion, celery and thyme and continue to sauté until softened, about 4 minutes.

3. Stir in chicken stock and soy sauce, scraping up brown bits from bottom of pan.

4. Stir in barley, reduce heat, cover and simmer for 10 to 15 minutes.

5. Stir in parsley, yogurt, salt and pepper until combined.

6. Garnish each serving with small pat of butter.

Makes 4 servings

VEGETARIAN

FRENCH

Black Bean
Burrito Salad w/ Avocado Dressing

INGREDIENTS

SALAD

- [ ] ¼ onion, diced or thinly sliced
- [ ] 4 cups (1 L) chopped romaine lettuce
- [ ] 1 cup (250 mL) black beans, drained and rinsed
- [ ] 1 cup (250 mL) cherry or grape tomatoes, halved
- [ ] 1 cup (250 mL) quinoa, cooked
- [ ] ½ cup (125 mL) shredded cheddar or Monterey Jack cheese
- [ ] ¼ cup (60 mL) fresh cilantro, chopped

DRESSING

- [ ] 1 small clove garlic, minced or pressed
- [ ] ½ avocado
- [ ] 2 tbsp (30 mL) lime juice
- [ ] ¼ tsp (1 mL) salt

VEGETARIAN

VEGAN

MEXICAN

Whoever said you can't make friends with salad definitely hasn't tried this one. Try scooping it up with corn chips or wrapping it in a whole-grain tortilla for a more hearty meal. The avocado dressing is also extremely versatile and works well as a sauce for French fries and as a spread on a sandwich.

1. Dressing: In food processor or blender, purée garlic, avocado, lime juice and salt until blended and smooth. Set aside.

2. In large bowl, toss together onion, lettuce, beans, tomatoes, quinoa, cheese and cilantro. Toss in dressing to coat.

Makes 2 servings

Chickpea falafel salad
w/ Tahini Dressing

INGREDIENTS
SALAD

- ☐ ¹/₂ cup (125 mL) uncooked bulgur
- ☐ 1 cup (250 mL) water or vegetable stock
- ☐ 2 tomatoes, diced
- ☐ 2 green onions, diced
- ☐ 1 bunch Italian parsley, stems removed and coarsely chopped
- ☐ ¹/₂ cup (125 mL) loosely packed fresh cilantro leaves, chopped
- ☐ ¹/₂ English cucumber, diced
- ☐ 1 can (14 oz/398 mL) chickpeas, drained and rinsed
- ☐ ¹/₂ cup (125 mL) crumbled feta cheese (optional)

DRESSING

- ☐ 2 cloves garlic, chopped
- ☐ ¹/₃ cup (75 mL) tahini (sesame seed paste)
- ☐ ¹/₃ cup (75 mL) water
- ☐ ¹/₄ cup (60 mL) lemon juice
- ☐ 1 tbsp (15 mL) liquid honey
- ☐ ¹/₂ tsp (2 mL) ground cumin
- ☐ ¹/₂ tsp (2 mL) salt

Falafel — that food you eat that is deep fried and soaks up garlicky dressing, yet somehow comes from a bean. As a "sometimes" food, sure, but for a cleaner, more everyday version that offers the same savoury Middle Eastern flavours, turn to this salad. It's easy on the waistline and surprisingly easy on the wallet, as well.

1. Dressing: In blender or food processor, purée garlic, tahini, water, lemon juice, honey, cumin and salt until blended and smooth.

2. Cover and refrigerate until ready to use.

3. In dry saucepan over medium-high heat, toast bulgur, stirring constantly, until fragrant, 2 to 3 minutes.

4. Stir in water and bring to a boil. Reduce heat, cover and simmer until tender and water has been absorbed, about 20 minutes.

5. Remove from heat, fluff with fork and let cool.

6. In large bowl, toss together bulgur, tomatoes, green onions, parsley, cilantro, cucumber and chickpeas. Toss in dressing to coat. Garnish with cheese (if using).

Makes 4 servings

VEGETARIAN

VEGAN

MIDDLE EASTERN

VARIATION:
For a more flavourful bulgur, use chicken or vegetable stock instead of water.

MAKE AHEAD:
Before adding dressing, refrigerate any unused salad in airtight container for up to 3 days. Transfer extra dressing to airtight container and refrigerate for up to 2 weeks.

salmon sushi salad
w/ Sesame Soy Dressing

INGREDIENTS

SALAD

- [ ] 3 cups (750 mL) chopped iceberg lettuce, torn into bite-sized pieces
- [ ] 5 oz (140 g) smoked salmon, sliced
- [ ] 2 green onions, thinly sliced on diagonal
- [ ] 1 avocado, cubed
- [ ] 1/2 cucumber, diced
- [ ] 1/2 cup (125 mL) carrot, grated
- [ ] 1/2 cup (125 mL) shelled edamame
- [ ] 1/4 cup (60 mL) coarsely chopped pickled ginger

DRESSING

- [ ] 2 tbsp (30 mL) soy sauce
- [ ] 2 tbsp (30 mL) rice vinegar
- [ ] 1 tbsp (15mL) water
- [ ] 1 tbsp (15 mL) toasted sesame oil
- [ ] 1 tbsp (15 mL) liquid honey

Rolling each individual sushi maki takes time if you're not an expert; this salad gives all the yummy flavours of sushi without the commitment. Try chopping the ingredients into different shapes and sizes or placing them in separate piles on the plate rather than mixed together in a salad. Remember, we eat with our eyes first, and this gives the dish more visual appeal.

1. Dressing: In small bowl, whisk soy sauce, vinegar, water, oil and honey until smooth and blended.

2. Cover and refrigerate until ready to use.

3. Divide lettuce between 2 serving bowls. Top with half each of the salmon, green onions, avocado, cucumber, carrot, edamame and ginger, then drizzle with half of the dressing.

Makes 2 servings

VARIATION:
Add 1/2 cup (125 mL) cooled cooked brown rice as a topping to the salad to make it a more filling meal.

ASIAN (JAPANESE)

Grilled Zucchini
& Corn Greek Salad

INGREDIENTS

SALAD

- [ ] 3 zucchini, sliced lengthwise
- [ ] $^1/_2$ tbsp (7 mL) canola oil (or cooking spray)
- [ ] 1 cup (250 mL) fresh cooked or canned corn kernels
- [ ] $^1/_4$ cup (60 mL) crumbled feta cheese
- [ ] $^1/_4$ cup (60 mL) torn fresh basil leaves

DRESSING

- [ ] 2 tbsp (30 mL) lemon juice
- [ ] 2 tbsp (30 mL) olive oil
- [ ] 1 tbsp (15 mL) liquid honey
- [ ] 1 tsp (5 mL) Dijon mustard
- [ ] Salt and pepper to taste

Zucchini and corn are at their peak of perfection late in the summer. This is one of those salads that is a cinch to whip up and pairs nicely with anything from fish to steak. Serving with a hearty slice of bread to soak up all the heart-healthy vinaigrette is strongly suggested.

1. Dressing: In small bowl, whisk lemon juice, oil, honey, mustard, salt and pepper until blended and smooth; cover and refrigerate until ready to use.

2. In shallow dish, gently toss zucchini with oil to coat.

3. Transfer to BBQ or indoor grill. Grill, turning once halfway through, until tender and slightly charred by grill rack, about 10 minutes.

4. With tongs, transfer to cutting board; let cool.

5. In large salad bowl, toss together corn, cheese, basil and dressing. Slice zucchini into bite-size chunks; gently fold into corn mixture.

Makes 4 servings

VEGETARIAN

GREEK

VARIATION:
Upgrade this side salad into a full meal by adding 2 cups of a cooked whole-grain such as quinoa, then topping it with toasted pine nuts or walnuts.

Roasted Garlic
& Kale Caesar

INGREDIENTS

SALAD

- [ ] One bunch lacinato or 'dinosaur" kale, ribs removed and sliced in ribbons
- [ ] ¼ cup (60 mL) grated Parmesan cheese

CROUTONS

- [ ] 2 or 3 slices day-old bread, torn in bite-size pieces (about 1 cup/250 mL)
- [ ] 1 tbsp (15 mL) olive oil

DRESSING

- [ ] 1 head garlic
- [ ] 3 tbsp (45 mL) olive oil, divided
- [ ] 2 tbsp (30 mL) lemon juice
- [ ] 2 tsp (10 mL) Dijon mustard
- [ ] ½ tsp (2 mL) salt

The kale Caesar is one spinoff from the superfood trend that's here to stay. Roasted garlic gives this dressing a creamy mouthfeel without extra calories from fat. Make a balanced meal from this dish by topping with a sunny side up egg or some shredded roasted chicken.

1. Croutons: Preheat the oven to 400°F (200°C).

2. On parchment paper–lined rimmed baking sheet, evenly spread bread. Lightly drizzle with oil.

3. Bake in oven, shaking pan once halfway through, until crisp and golden, about 5 minutes.

4. Transfer to rack. Let cool.

5. Dressing: Keep the oven at 400°F (200°C).

6. With sharp knife, trim tip from garlic head to expose tops of individual cloves.

7. Set garlic base on square of foil and drizzle 1 tablespoon (15 mL) oil into sliced tip between cloves. Gather foil corners up over tip and twist tightly to close.

8. Bake in oven until tender and fragrant, about 30 minutes.

9. Remove foil and let cool.

10. Squeeze garlic head at base to pop out cloves into food processor or blender.

11. Add remaining olive oil, lemon juice, mustard and salt. Purée until emulsified and smooth.

12. In large salad bowl with hands, toss together kale and dressing, massaging dressing into leaves; top with croutons and cheese.

Makes 4 servings

TIP:
You can refrigerate roasted garlic for 2 to 3 days before use, or purchase it already roasted at the deli counter in many grocery stores.

VARIATION:
Make a vegan version of this salad by replacing the Parmesan cheese with nutritional yeast, and throwing in some toasted almonds along with the croutons.

Thai Chicken Salad
w/ Peanut Dressing

VEGAN

ASIAN (THAI)

INGREDIENTS

SALAD

- [ ] 6 oz (170 g) boneless skinless chicken breast
- [ ] 2 carrots, grated
- [ ] 2 green onions, thinly sliced on diagonal
- [ ] 1/2 English cucumber, sliced
- [ ] 1/2 small sweet red, orange or yellow pepper, sliced
- [ ] 1/4 cup (60 mL) fresh cilantro leaves, finely diced, divided
- [ ] 2 tbsp (30 mL) crushed salted toasted peanuts (optional)

DRESSING

- [ ] 1 clove garlic, chopped
- [ ] 1/2-inch (1 cm) piece fresh ginger, minced
- [ ] 2 tbsp (30 mL) packed brown sugar
- [ ] 2 tbsp (30 mL) creamy natural peanut butter
- [ ] 2 tbsp (30 mL) sesame oil
- [ ] 1 tbsp (15 mL) rice vinegar
- [ ] 1 tbsp (15 mL) lime juice
- [ ] 2 tsp (10 mL) soy sauce
- [ ] 1/2 tsp (10 mL) red pepper flakes or Asian hot sauce

Crispy, crunchy vegetables with some lean protein and a creamy mess of spicy, salty-sweet dressing makes for an enticing anytime meal. While this salad is best when it's fresh and still slightly warm from the chicken, you can substitute more rigid vegetables that will stand up to being refrigerated in the tangy peanut dressing for a couple of days (think cabbage, jicama, carrots and broccoli). The dressing also makes a great sauce for noodles or mixed with tuna for sandwiches — not that you'll have any left over.

1. In non-stick pan over medium heat, cover and cook chicken, stirring occasionally, until cooked through and no longer pink in centre, 8 to 10 minutes.

2. Set aside to rest for 5 to 10 minutes while assembling the rest of the salad.

3. Dressing: Meanwhile, in food processor or blender, purée garlic, ginger, brown sugar, peanut butter, oil, vinegar, lime juice, soy sauce and red pepper flakes.

4. Slice the cooked chicken breast thinly against the grain and transfer to large salad bowl. Toss in dressing and let marinate for about 5 minutes.

5. Toss in carrots, green onions, cucumber, sweet pepper and about half of the cilantro to coat.

6. Garnish with remaining cilantro and peanuts (if using).

Makes 2 servings

VARIATIONS:
For a meatless vegan meal, omit the chicken and replace with 1/2 cup (125 mL) shelled edamame or chunks of pan-fried tofu.

Mandarin, Almond
& Quinoa Salad

INGREDIENTS

SALAD

- ☐ ¹/₂ cup (125 mL) uncooked quinoa
- ☐ 1 cup (250 mL) water or vegetable stock
- ☐ ¹/₂ cup (125 mL) frozen baby peas
- ☐ 1 can (11 oz / 312 g) mandarin oranges, drained, syrup reserved
- ☐ ¹/₂ English cucumber, chopped in bite-size pieces
- ☐ ¹/₄ red onion, chopped in bite-size pieces
- ☐ ¹/₄ cup (60 mL) chopped fresh cilantro
- ☐ ¹/₄ cup (60 mL) toasted sliced almonds

DRESSING

- ☐ 2 tbsp (30 mL) rice vinegar
- ☐ 2 tbsp (30 mL) canola oil
- ☐ 2 tbsp (30 mL) reserved mandarin orange syrup
- ☐ 1 tbsp (15 mL) sesame oil
- ☐ 1 tbsp (15 mL) soy sauce
- ☐ 1 tsp (5 mL) hot sweet mustard

This is a great recipe for a busy weekday meal, potluck dinner or summer BBQ because it holds up well in the refrigerator and seems to only get better with time. Grilled fish or tofu makes the perfect accompaniment to this salad.

1. In saucepan over medium-high heat, toast quinoa, stirring, until fragrant, 2 to 3 minutes.

2. Stir in water and bring to a boil. Reduce heat, cover and simmer until tender and grains are edged with white, about 15 minutes.

3. Remove from heat, uncover and fluff with fork; stir in peas and let cool.

4. Dressing: In nonreactive bowl, whisk vinegar, canola oil, reserved syrup, sesame oil, soy sauce and mustard until blended and smooth.

5. Cover and refrigerate until ready to use.

6. In large salad bowl, toss together quinoa and peas, oranges, cucumber, onion, and cilantro. Toss in dressing to coat. Sprinkle almonds overtop.

Makes 4 servings

VARIATIONS:
Add more flavour to the quinoa by cooking it with chicken or vegetable stock instead of water.
For more protein, replace peas with thawed frozen shelled edamame beans.

MAKE AHEAD:
Transfer any extra dressing to airtight container and refrigerate for up to 2 weeks. Cover and refrigerate any leftover salad for up to 3 days.

VEGETARIAN

VEGAN

ASIAN

Edamame ramen salad
& ORANGE SESAME DRESSING

INGREDIENTS

SALAD

- [ ] 2 packages (each 3 oz/85 g) ramen noodles, coarsely crushed
- [ ] 1/2 cup (125 mL) sliced almonds
- [ ] 1 avocado, diced
- [ ] 1 can (11 oz/312 g) mandarin oranges, drained, syrup reserved
- [ ] 2 cups (500 mL) cabbage, thinly sliced
- [ ] 1 cup (250 mL) frozen shelled edamame, thawed
- [ ] 1/2 cup (125 mL) green onions, sliced
- [ ] 1/2 cup (125 mL) fresh cilantro, chopped

DRESSING

- [ ] 1/2 cup (125 mL) sunflower oil
- [ ] 1/3 cup (75 mL) reserved mandarin orange syrup
- [ ] 1/3 cup (75 mL) rice vinegar
- [ ] 1 tbsp (15 mL) soy sauce
- [ ] 1 tsp (5 mL) sesame oil
- [ ] Salt and pepper to taste

A fresh take on a potluck staple, this salad is an inexpensive crowd-pleaser. Always remember to discard the seasoning packets from the ramen noodle packages since they're full of nasty ingredients such as sodium and artificial additives.

1. Preheat the oven to 425°F (220°C).

2. Arrange noodles and almonds evenly on parchment paper–lined rimmed baking sheet.

3. Bake in oven, gently shaking pan several times to prevent burning, until noodles are fragrant and toasted, 5 to 8 minutes.

4. Transfer to rack. Let cool.

5. Dressing: In large salad bowl, whisk sunflower oil, reserved syrup, vinegar, soy sauce, sesame oil, salt and pepper.

6. Toss in avocado, oranges, cabbage, edamame, onion and cilantro to coat.

7. Toss in reserved noodles and almonds to coat.

Makes 6 servings

VEGETARIAN

VEGAN

ASIAN

Roasted Vegetable
& Quinoa Salad w/ Honey Mustard Dressing

INGREDIENTS

SALAD

- [ ] 4 cloves garlic, crushed
- [ ] 2 carrots, sliced in rounds
- [ ] 1 parsnip, sliced in rounds
- [ ] 1 red onion, chopped
- [ ] 1 small fennel bulb, chopped
- [ ] 1/2 lb (225 g) Brussels sprouts, halved
- [ ] 3 tbsp (45 mL) olive oil
- [ ] 1 tbsp (15 mL) brown sugar
- [ ] Salt and pepper to taste
- [ ] 1 cup (250 mL) quinoa, cooked and cooled

DRESSING

- [ ] 1/2 cup (125 mL) plain Greek yogurt
- [ ] 1/4 cup (60 mL) liquid honey
- [ ] 2 tbsp (30 mL) prepared mustard
- [ ] 1 tbsp (15 mL) lemon juice
- [ ] 1/2 tsp (2 mL) salt
- [ ] 1/4 tsp (1 mL) pepper

Roasting vegetables caramelizes their naturally occurring sugars, making them taste sweeter and nuttier. A great salad for using up vegetables before they get to the compost bin, this can be made even more special by adding crumbled goat cheese and your favourite fresh herbs.

1. Preheat oven to 400°F (200°C).

2. In large bowl, toss together garlic, carrots, parsnip, onion, fennel and Brussels sprouts with olive oil to coat.

3. Spread on rimmed baking sheet and sprinkle with brown sugar, salt and pepper.

4. Bake in oven, stirring occasionally, until tender and golden, 20 minutes.

5. Transfer to rack. Let cool for 10 to 15 minutes.

6. Dressing: In small bowl, whisk yogurt, honey, mustard, lemon juice, salt and pepper until blended and smooth.

7. Cover and refrigerate until ready to use.

8. In large salad bowl, toss together quinoa, vegetable mixture and dressing to taste.

Makes 4 servings

VEGETARIAN

NORTH AMERICAN

VARIATION:
Add more flavour to the quinoa by cooking it with chicken or vegetable stock instead of water.

MAKE AHEAD:
Transfer extra Dressing to an airtight container and refrigerate for up to 1 week.

spinach, strawberry
& Feta Salad

INGREDIENTS

SALAD

- ☐ ¹/₂ lb (225 g) baby spinach
- ☐ ¹/₂ lb (225 g) fresh strawberries, hulled and sliced in half lengthwise
- ☐ ¹/₂ cup (125 mL) crumbled feta cheese, divided

DRESSING

- ☐ ¹/₄ cup (60 mL) olive oil
- ☐ ¹/₄ tbsp (45 mL) balsamic vinegar
- ☐ 1 tbsp (15 mL) toasted sesame seeds
- ☐ ¹/₂ tbsp (7 mL) liquid honey
- ☐ ¹/₄ tsp (1 mL) cinnamon
- ☐ Salt and pepper to taste

Sweet strawberries are enhanced by the salty feta, and the baby spinach is a healthful vehicle for the bold balsamic vinaigrette. Try doubling the ingredients for the dressing and refrigerate half in an airtight glass jar for later use.

1. Dressing: In small bowl, whisk oil, vinegar, sesame seeds, honey, cinnamon, salt and pepper.

2. In large salad bowl, toss together spinach, strawberries and three-quarters of the cheese. Toss in dressing.

3. Garnish with remaining cheese.

Makes 4 servings

VEGETARIAN

MEDITERRANEAN

VARIATION:
You can add thin slices of red onion to this salad or replace the strawberries with another fruit such as sliced pear or apple, or other berries. You can also use goat cheese instead of feta and replace the sesame seeds with sunflower seeds.

Broccoli, Grape
& Pasta Salad w/ Greek Yogurt Dressing

INGREDIENTS

SALAD

- [ ] 4 large leaves iceberg lettuce
- [ ] 8 oz (4 cups or 1L) bowtie pasta, cooked, drained and cooled
- [ ] 1 head broccoli, finely chopped
- [ ] $^1/_2$ small red onion, diced
- [ ] 2 cups (500 mL) seedless red grapes, halved
- [ ] $^1/_2$ cup (125 mL) salted sunflower seeds

DRESSING

- [ ] $^1/_4$ cup (60 mL) Greek yogurt
- [ ] $^1/_4$ cup (60 mL) mayonnaise
- [ ] 2 tbsp (30 mL) red wine vinegar
- [ ] 1 tbsp (15 mL) chopped parsley
- [ ] 1 tsp (5 mL) liquid honey
- [ ] Salt and pepper to taste

This is a great salad to make ahead on a Sunday for a busy week. It holds up well and its tangy flavour only improves after a couple of days in the fridge. Try preportioning this batch of salad into single-serve containers for quick and balanced midweek lunches.

1. Dressing: In bowl, whisk yogurt, mayonnaise, vinegar, parsley, honey, salt and pepper until combined.

2. In large bowl, toss together pasta, broccoli, onion, grapes and sunflower seeds. Toss in dressing to coat.

3. On each of 4 plates, place 1 lettuce leaf, inside up, to form 'salad bowl."

4. Divide salad among 4 leaves.

Makes 4 servings

VARIATION:
Sprinkle crumbled, crisp bacon bits over top to make this salad a meaty meal.

VEGETARIAN

NORTH AMERICAN

Grape Tomato
Caprese Salad

INGREDIENTS

SALAD

- [ ] 2 cups (500 mL) grape tomatoes, halved
- [ ] ½ cup (125 mL) fresh basil leaves, torn
- [ ] 1 cup (250 mL) small bocconcini mozzarella cheese, drained and halved
- [ ] Salt and pepper to taste

DRESSING

- [ ] 1 small clove garlic, minced or pressed
- [ ] 2 tbsp (30 mL) olive oil
- [ ] 1 tbsp (15 mL) white wine vinegar

VEGETARIAN

ITALIAN

Caprese salad is a staple Italian dish: tomato, mozzarella cheese and basil — arguably one of the best flavour combinations known to the culinary world! This spin on the traditional caprese uses grape tomatoes (which just happen to last forever in the fridge), and can be eaten with a spoon or piled high on thick slices of Italian bread.

1. Dressing: Whisk garlic, oil and vinegar until blended and smooth.

2. In large salad bowl, toss together tomatoes, basil, cheese, salt and pepper; toss in dressing to coat.

Makes 2 servings

VARIATIONS:
If fresh basil isn't available, add 1 tbsp (15 mL) store-bought pesto to dressing instead.
If bocconcini isn't available, replace it with bite-size chunks of any fresh mozzarella cheese.

Classic Creamy Hummus

INGREDIENTS

- [ ] 1/4 cup (60 mL) tahini (sesame seed paste), divided
- [ ] 1/4 cup (60 mL) lemon juice
- [ ] 1 can (14 oz/398 mL) chickpeas, drained and rinsed, divided
- [ ] 1 small clove garlic, minced
- [ ] 1/2 tsp (2 mL) ground cumin
- [ ] 1/2 tsp (2 mL) salt
- [ ] 2 tbsp (30 mL) water
- [ ] 2 tbsp (30 mL) olive oil (optional)
- [ ] 1/2 tsp (2 mL) paprika (optional)

PITA CHIPS

- [ ] 3 or 4 pitas, each cut in 8 triangles
- [ ] Cooking spray
- [ ] 1/2 tsp (2 mL) salt

The popularity of this Middle Eastern dish has skyrocketed for good reason. It's creamy, versatile and incredibly good for you. I suggest having some in the fridge at all times — for a dip with snacks or a spread, or a straight-up spoonful when you need it.

1. Pita Chips: Preheat oven to 400°F (200°C).

2. Arrange pitas in single layer on rimmed baking sheet, spritz with cooking spray and sprinkle with salt.

3. Bake in oven, turning once halfway through, for about 7 minutes.

4. Transfer to cooling rack. Let cool.

5. In food processor or blender, purée half of the tahini with lemon juice until smooth and almost whipped.

6. Add half of the chickpeas, garlic, cumin and salt; purée until blended and smooth, 2 to 3 minutes.

7. Scrape down side of food processor. Add remaining chickpeas and purée for 2 to 3 minutes.

8. Scrape down side of food processor. Cover and, with processor running, carefully pour in water and purée for 1 to 2 minutes.

9. Scrape down the sides again, add remaining tahini to the processor and purée for another 1 to 2 minutes to ensure it's completely smooth.

10. Transfer to serving bowl. Drizzle with oil (if using) and sprinkle with paprika (if using). Serve with Pita Chips on side.

Makes 2 cups (500 mL)

VARIATION:
Process the hummus with these additions for 2 to 3 extra minutes to make sure it's creamy.
ROASTED RED PEPPER HUMMUS: Add a 12 oz (350 mL) jar of roasted red peppers (drained) and 1/2 tsp (3 mL) of cayenne pepper.
JALAPENO & CILANTRO HUMMUS: Add 1 jalapeño pepper, seeded and diced, and 1/4 cup (60 mL) diced cilantro leaves.

SOUTHWESTERN BLACK BEAN HUMMUS:
Swap the chickpeas for an equal amount of black beans and add 1/2 teaspoon cayenne to the processor.

VEGETARIAN | VEGAN | MIDDLE EASTERN

Tomato & Basil
Bruschetta w/ Toasted Baguette

INGREDIENTS

- [ ] ¹/₂ baguette
- [ ] 4 tbsp (60mL) olive oil, divided
- [ ] ¹/₂ cup (125 mL) packed fresh basil leaves
- [ ] 3 or 4 Roma tomatoes, halved lengthwise, seeded and diced
- [ ] 1 large clove garlic, minced
- [ ] ¹/₂ tsp (2 mL) salt, divided

Fresh and simple, bruschetta is the perfect summertime patio snack. This topping is best served with the toasted baguette, but it can also be served on a baked potato or even as a salad dressing.

1. Preheat oven to broil.

2. Cut baguette on diagonal into 8 same-size slices.

3. Arrange in single layer on rimmed baking sheet and drizzle with roughly half of the olive oil. Set aside.

4. On cutting board, stack basil leaves, a few at a time, then tightly roll and finely slice into thin threads.

5. In bowl, toss together basil, tomatoes, garlic, the remaining oil and half of the salt. Set aside.

6. Broil baguette on top rack in oven, turning once halfway through and watching to prevent burning, until toasted and golden.

7. Remove from heat and sprinkle with remaining salt. Divide basil mixture evenly among baguette slices.

Makes 4 servings

VEGETARIAN

VEGAN

ITALIAN

Chunky Guacamole

VEGETARIAN

VEGAN

MEXICAN

INGREDIENTS

- [ ] 2 avocados, cut in halves and pits removed
- [ ] 3 tbsp (45 mL) lime juice
- [ ] ¹/₂ jalapeño pepper, seeded and minced
- [ ] ¹/₄ red onion, diced
- [ ] 2 tbsp (30 mL) fresh cilantro, minced
- [ ] 1 tsp (5 mL) salt

Avocados are like cream cheese from nature, with super-creamy texture, lots of fibre and full of heart-healthy fats. Try making a batch of this to snack on during exams or when you're hanging out with friends. Serve it as a dip with low-sodium whole-grain tortilla chips and sliced vegetables.

1. Use the bowl of a large spoon to cleanly scoop avocado flesh from skin. With cut side down on cutting board, slice flesh into cubes and place in a bowl.

2. Gently toss avocado cubes with lime juice to coat; fold in jalapeño, onion, cilantro and salt.

Makes about 1 ¹/₂ cups (375 mL)

VARIATIONS:
- For a milder flavour, swap a green or sweet Vidalia onion for the red onion.
- Add a minced clove of garlic for a punch of flavour.
- Make it extra hot and spicy by mincing and using the whole jalapeño and even a few of the seeds.

spicy Mango salsa

INGREDIENTS

- [ ] 3 or 4 ripe mangos or 2 cups (500 mL) thawed frozen diced mango
- [ ] 1 small jalapeño pepper, seeded and minced
- [ ] 1/2 sweet red pepper, diced
- [ ] 1/4 red onion, diced
- [ ] 3 tbsp (45 mL) minced fresh cilantro
- [ ] 3 tbsp (45 mL) lime juice
- [ ] 1/2 tsp (2 mL) salt

Sweet and spicy mango salsa is a colourful addition to any meal. Serve as a topping for grilled fish or meat, or as a dip with whole-grain tortilla chips.

1. In large bowl, toss together mangos, jalapeño, red pepper, onion, cilantro, lime juice and salt to coat.

2. Let stand at room temperature for 5 minutes before serving.

Makes 2 1/2 cups (625 mL)

VARIATIONS:
- For a milder flavour, swap green or sweet Vidalia onion for the red onion.
- Replace the mango with another fruit such as pineapple or blueberries.
- Make it extra hot and spicy by adding a few of the jalapeño seeds.

VEGETARIAN

VEGAN

TEX-MEX

Baked Sweet
Potato Fries w/ Spicy Mayo

INGREDIENTS

- ☐ Cooking spray, for pan
- ☐ 2 unpeeled sweet potatoes, cut in French fries
- ☐ 1 tbsp (15 mL) cornstarch
- ☐ ¹/₂ tsp (2 mL) salt

SAUCE

- ☐ ¹/₂ cup (125 mL) mayonnaise
- ☐ 1 tbsp (15 mL) store-bought hot sauce

Sweet potato fries are the definitive comfort food. These make an excellent side for sandwiches or burgers, or on their own as a first-rate study snack

1. Preheat oven to 425°F (220°C).

2. Coat rimmed baking sheet with cooking spray. Set aside.

3. With paper towel, pat sweet potatoes dry.

4. Transfer to large resealable plastic bag. Sprinkle cornstarch and salt over potatoes, seal bag and shake to coat.

5. Spread on baking sheet. Bake in oven, turning once halfway through, until golden and crisp, 20 to 30 minutes.

6. Sauce: In small bowl, whisk mayonnaise with hot sauce until blended and smooth. Serve on side with hot fries.

Makes 2 cups (500 mL)

VARIATIONS:
Instead of plain salt on your fries, try one of these:
- 2 tsp (10 mL) ground cumin
- 2 tsp (10 mL) cinnamon
- 1 tbsp (15 mL) curry powder

VEGETARIAN

VEGAN

CENTRAL AMERICAN

Baked Zucchini fries
w/ Marinara Sauce

INGREDIENTS

- [ ] ³/₄ cup (175 mL) panko bread crumbs
- [ ] ¹/₄ cup (60 mL) Parmesan cheese, grated
- [ ] 3 or 4 small zucchini, halved and seeded
- [ ] 2 egg whites, whisked
- [ ] Cooking spray
- [ ] ¹/₂ cup (125 mL) store-bought marinara sauce

Zucchini fries are a perfect snack. The flesh inside is creamy and the outside is crispy and salty; it tastes like junk food but without any of the nutritional pitfalls. This is a modern take on traditional Italian flavors that is sure to satisfy.

1. Preheat oven to 425°F (215°C).

2. In shallow dish, stir bread crumbs with cheese. Set aside.

3. Cut each zucchini half lengthwise into 4 or 5 strips. Transfer to paper towel and gently pat dry.

4. Toss the zucchini fries into the beaten egg whites. Roll each strip in bread crumb mixture.

5. Arrange on parchment paper–lined rimmed baking sheet. Generously coat zucchini with cooking spray.

6. Bake in oven, turning once halfway through, for 20 minutes.

7. Serve marinara sauce, for dipping, on side.

Makes 4 servings

TIP:
Use the bowl of a small spoon to scoop out seeds from halved zucchini.

VEGETARIAN

ITALIAN

No-Bake Energy Balls

INGREDIENTS

- [ ] 1 cup (250 mL) rolled oats
- [ ] ¹/₂ cup (125 mL) preferred nut butter
- [ ] ¹/₂ cup (125 mL) ground flaxseed or chia seeds
- [ ] ¹/₂ cup (125 mL) semisweet chocolate chips
- [ ] ¹/₃ cup (75 mL) liquid honey or maple syrup
- [ ] 1 tsp (5 mL) vanilla extract
- [ ] ¹/₂ tsp (2 mL) cinnamon

VEGETARIAN

VEGAN

NORTH AMERICAN

Energy balls are the best cookie alternative out there. These are easy to make for a perfect breakfast on the run or a quick study snack. If you'd prefer a cookie-shaped energy bite instead of a ball, use the tines of a fork to flatten these before freezing them, or press all of the dough into a greased pan, then cut it into bars.

1. In bowl with fork, stir together oats, nut butter, flaxseed, chocolate chips, honey and vanilla until thoroughly mixed and coated.

2. With hands, form into balls of about 2 tbsp (30 mL) each and transfer to parchment paper–lined rimmed baking sheet that fits flat in your freezer.

3. Cover with plastic wrap and freeze for about 1 hour or until firm and set. Store prepared energy balls in a resealable plastic container in the fridge for up to 5 days, or freeze for longer storage.

Makes 10 to 12 balls

TIP:
If oat mixture is too sticky to handle, cover and refrigerate for about 30 minutes before forming into balls.

VARIATIONS:
• Try different combinations of nut butters, syrups and flavour extracts, and replace chocolate chips with chopped dried fruit. Some great combinations are:
sunflower seed butter, sweetened dried cranberries and liquid honey, almond butter, shredded coconut and dried blueberries peanut butter, raisins and maple syrup.

steamed & salted Edamame

INGREDIENTS

- [ ] About 24 cups (6 L) water
- [ ] 1 tbsp (15 mL) coarse salt + more for sprinkling
- [ ] 2 cups (500 mL) fresh or frozen edamame in pods

Soybeans, unlike other beans, are a complete source of protein. Quick to throw together, this snack is good warm or cool, and pretty perfect for after school.

1. In large pot over medium-high heat, bring water and 1 tbsp (15 mL) of the salt to a rolling boil.

2. Add edamame, cover and cook until tender and pods are loosened, 5 to 10 minutes.

3. Drain. Transfer to large bowl and sprinkle with salt.

4. Serve with an extra bowl for discarding the pods.

Makes 2 servings

VEGETARIAN

VEGAN

ASIAN (JAPANESE)

Spinach & Artichoke Dip
& Tortilla Chips

INGREDIENTS

- [ ] 8 oz (226 g) brick light cream cheese, cut into cubes
- [ ] 1 cup frozen spinach, thawed and chopped
- [ ] 1 can (14 oz/398 mL) artichokes in brine, drained and chopped
- [ ] 2 cloves garlic, minced
- [ ] 1/2 cup (125 mL) plain Greek yogurt
- [ ] 1/4 cup (60 mL) mayonnaise
- [ ] 1 cup (125 mL) shredded mozzarella
- [ ] 1/3 cup (80 mL) grated Parmesan cheese
- [ ] 1/2 tsp (3 mL) crushed red pepper
- [ ] 1/4 tsp (3 mL) salt
- [ ] 6 small whole-grain tortillas

Frozen spinach and canned artichoke make this dip super-easy, and it tastes as good as at a restaurant. Serve piping hot with tortilla chips and any other dippers you enjoy.

1. Place cream cheese in a medium, microwave-safe bowl and microwave on high for about 30 seconds, just until soft.

2. Stir in the spinach, artichokes, garlic, Greek yogurt, mayonnaise, mozzarella, Parmesan, crushed red pepper and salt until mixed well.

3. Transfer the dip to a greased casserole dish, using a spatula to evenly spread.

4. Bake in a preheated oven at 350°F while preparing the tortilla chips.

5. Cut tortillas into triangles and place them on a parchment-lined baking pan. Bake for a total of 12 to 15 minutes or until golden and crisp, flipping halfway through.

6. Serve the dip warm with tortilla chips and optional crudités, such as carrots, celery, and grape tomatoes.

Makes 6-8 servings

VEGETARIAN

NORTH AMERICAN

kimchi fries

INGREDIENTS

- [ ] 1 lb (450 g) frozen low-sodium French fries
- [ ] 1 tbsp (15 mL) sugar
- [ ] 1 tbsp (15 mL) white vinegar
- [ ] 1 tbsp (15 mL) soy sauce
- [ ] 1/2 cup (125 mL) kimchi
- [ ] 1 tbsp (15 mL) canola oil
- [ ] 1 cup (250 mL) shredded white cheddar cheese
- [ ] 1/2 cup (125 mL) cilantro leaves
- [ ] 2 tsp (10 mL) sesame oil
- [ ] Sesame seeds to garnish

Korean-style street food is available in nearly every metropolis for good reason; caramelized kimchi with cheddar cheese over French fries is a fusion food that's here to stay. Try using low-sodium, frozen French fries for ease of preparing this dish, and serve alongside some smoky grilled protein.

1. Prepare the French fries by baking according to package directions. While the French fries are baking, whisk together the sugar, vinegar and soy sauce in a medium bowl. Add the kimchi and reserve.

2. Heat a frying pan over medium-high heat. Pour in the oil followed by the kimchi mixture, and caramelize the kimchi for about 5 minutes.

3. Scatter the French fries over a platter, top with shredded cheddar cheese, hot kimchi, cilantro leaves and drizzle with sesame oil and seeds.

Makes 4 servings

VEGETARIAN

ASIAN (KOREAN)

Crispy Buffalo
ROASTED CHICKPEAS

INGREDIENTS

- [ ] 2 cans (each 14 oz / 398 mL) chickpeas
- [ ] Cooking spray
- [ ] 2 tbsp (30 mL) chili powder

This is a fantastic alternative to greasy chips for a salty snack! Canned chickpeas are an economical choice (usually under a dollar a can) and packed with nutrition. Keep some on hand in your locker, car and gym bag for emergency snacks.

1. Line a baking sheet with paper towel. Drain and rinse the chickpeas and spread across the paper towel, blotting them dry with extra paper towel if needed.

2. Remove the paper towel and lightly mist with the cooking spray. Sprinkle the chickpeas with the chili powder and gently toss on the pan to coat.

3. Bake in a preheated oven at 400°F (200°C), shaking the pan every 10 minutes or so to toss.

4. Remove from the oven after 30 to 40 minutes and allow them to cool completely on the pan before storing in an airtight container.

Makes 6-8 servings

VARIATIONS:
- ½ tbsp (7 mL) cinnamon & 1 ½ tbsp (23 mL) sugar
- 2 tbsp (30 mL) curry powder
- 1 tsp (5 mL) sea salt

VEGETARIAN

VEGAN

INDIAN

sandwiches & Burgers

smashed Chickpea
Salad Sandwich

INGREDIENTS

- ☐ 1 can (14 oz / 398 mL) chickpeas, drained and rinsed
- ☐ 1 stalk celery, diced
- ☐ 1 clove garlic, pressed
- ☐ 1/4 cup (60 mL) red onion, finely diced
- ☐ 1/4 cup (60 mL) sweet red pepper, finely diced
- ☐ 3 tbsp (45 mL) mayonnaise
- ☐ 1 tbsp (15 mL) lemon juice
- ☐ 1 tsp (5 mL) prepared mustard
- ☐ 1/2 tsp (2 mL) dried dill, crumbled (or 2 tsp/10 mL fresh, minced)
- ☐ 1/2 tsp (2 mL) sea salt
- ☐ Pepper to taste
- ☐ 4 slices whole-grain bread
- ☐ 8 slices cucumber
- ☐ 4 slices tomato
- ☐ 4 leaves lettuce

Smashed chickpeas, crisp veggies and a creamy sauce make this a great topping for crackers or stuffing for sandwiches and wraps. The fibre and protein from the chickpeas is sure to keep you feeling full for hours. Since the flavour only gets better, this filling is a great make-ahead dish to keep in the fridge.

1. In large bowl with potato masher or fork, break up chickpeas into coarse pieces.

2. Stir in celery, garlic, onion, red pepper, mayonnaise, lemon juice, mustard, dill, salt and pepper.

3. Divide chickpea mixture between 2 slices of bread.

4. Top each with cucumber, tomato, lettuce and another slice of bread.

Makes 2 sandwiches

VARIATIONS:
- Make a vegan version by using vegan mayonnaise.
- Omit salt and stir 2 tbsp (30mL) finely crumbled feta cheese into chickpea mixture.
- Omit mustard, substitute fresh cilantro for dill and add 1 tsp (5 mL) curry powder to chickpea mixture.

VEGETARIAN

VEGAN

NORTH AMERICAN

Turkey & Pickled Veg
Deli Sandwich

INGREDIENTS

PICKLES

- [ ] 2 cloves garlic, smashed
- [ ] 1 radish, finely sliced in rounds
- [ ] 1/2 stalk celery, finely sliced on diagonal
- [ ] 1/2 carrot, finely sliced on diagonal
- [ ] 1/2 jalapeño pepper, seeded and finely sliced crosswise
- [ ] 1/4 sweet red pepper, finely sliced in strips
- [ ] 1/4 red onion, finely sliced in strips
- [ ] 2 tbsp (30 mL) sugar
- [ ] 1 cup (250 mL) vinegar

SANDWICH

- [ ] 2 thick slices pumpernickel bread
- [ ] 1 tbsp (15 mL) mayonnaise
- [ ] 3 oz (85 g) natural or low-sodium deli turkey
- [ ] 1 1/2 oz (40 g) Swiss or Emmental cheese

Pickled vegetables amplify the flavours in this delectable deli-style sandwich. Try purchasing the least-processed turkey available in the deli such as a whole roasted breast. Lower in sodium and meatier in texture, it will not only be more healthful but it will boost the flavour of the dressing.

1. Pickles: In bowl, stir together garlic, radish, celery, carrot, jalapeño, red pepper and onion. Set aside.

2. In microwaveable glass measure, stir sugar into vinegar. Microwave on high for 2 minutes. Pour over garlic mixture.

3. Cover and refrigerate for 10 to 15 minutes, before using.

4. Spread 1 bread slice with mayonnaise, top with turkey, pickles, cheese and remaining bread slice; cut in half on diagonal.

Makes 1 serving

TIP:
To slice vegetables ultrafine, you can use a mandoline, but take extra care with the sharp blades!

JEWISH AMERICAN

pesto Tuna
& Roasted Red Pepper Sandwich

INGREDIENTS

- ☐ 1/2 cup (125 mL) store-bought roasted red peppers, drained
- ☐ 1 can (6 oz/170 g) water-packed skipjack tuna, drained
- ☐ 2 tbsp (30 mL) diced red onion
- ☐ 1 tbsp (15 mL) mayonnaise
- ☐ 1 tbsp (15 mL) store-bought pesto
- ☐ 4 slices sourdough or multigrain bread
- ☐ 1 cup (250 mL) loosely packed arugula or spinach

Basil pesto makes this sandwich far from boring, and roasted red peppers are a hidden gem in grocery stores; the two combine to make a superb tuna sandwich. Canned skipjack was chosen for this recipe because it boasts the health benefits of omega-3 fatty acids but is lower in mercury — and price — than the larger albacore tuna.

1. With paper towel, pat red peppers dry. Set aside.

2. In bowl with fork, stir together tuna, onion, mayonnaise and pesto. Divide mixture between 2 bread slices.

3. Divide red peppers and arugula between each; top each with 1 bread slice.

Makes 2 servings

ITALIAN

SANDWICH

INGREDIENTS

CRANBERRY SAUCE

- ☐ 1 cup (250 mL) fresh or thawed frozen cranberries
- ☐ 1/2 cup (125 mL) water
- ☐ 1/4 cup (60 mL) sugar

SANDWICH

- ☐ 2 thick slices multigrain bread
- ☐ 1 tbsp (15 mL) mayonnaise
- ☐ 1/2 cup (125 mL) loosely packed spinach or lettuce
- ☐ 3 oz (85 g) natural or low-sodium deli turkey
- ☐ 1 thin slice of red onion
- ☐ 1 1/2 oz (40 g) cream cheese or goat cheese

This may be a fantastic way to use up the leftovers from turkey dinner, but it's easy enough to make all year round. Any sweet-tart cranberry sauce left over from this recipe is great with pork, chicken or even whisked with a bit of olive oil for a salad dressing.

1. Sauce: In small saucepan over medium-high heat, stir together cranberries, water and sugar.

2. Bring to a simmer and cook until cranberries are softened and skins are split, 5 to 10 minutes.

3. Remove from heat. Let cool for 10 to 15 minutes.

4. On 1 bread slice, spread mayonnaise. Top with spinach, turkey, sauce, onion.

5. Spread cheese on the remaining slice of bread and top the sandwich with it. Cut in half on diagonal.

Makes 1 serving

> **TIP:**
> It's not essential to make cranberry sauce from scratch, but it is super-easy and extra cranberries store really well in the freezer until you make another batch. You can use canned cranberry sauce in this sandwich, instead, if that's what you have on hand.

ENGLISH

Jerk Spiced Lentil
Sloppy Joes

VEGETARIAN

VEGAN

JAMAICAN

INGREDIENTS

- [ ] 2 tbsp (30 mL) coconut oil
- [ ] 1 yellow onion, diced
- [ ] 1-inch (2.5 cm) piece fresh ginger, grated
- [ ] 1 can (15 oz/425 g) lentils, drained and rinsed
- [ ] 1 tbsp (15 mL) jerk seasoning
- [ ] 1 can (28 oz/796 mL) low-sodium crushed tomatoes, with juice
- [ ] 2 tbsp (30 mL) liquid honey or packed brown sugar
- [ ] 1 tbsp (15 mL) lemon juice
- [ ] 4 hamburger buns, toasted or broiled
- [ ] 1 cup (250 mL) packed baby spinach

Jerk is to Jamaica as curry is to India: a blend of traditional spices with a history and flavour unique to the culture and so very special. Search online for a recipe for jerk seasoning to mix your own, or purchase a prepared mix for ease and convenience.

1. In saucepan over medium-high heat, melt oil. Sauté onion until translucent, about 4 to 5 minutes.

2. Add ginger and lentils. Sauté for 3 to 4 minutes.

3. Stir in jerk seasoning. Sauté for 1 minute.

4. Stir in tomatoes. Cook, stirring, until heated through.

5. Reduce heat and simmer, stirring occasionally, for 5 minutes.

6. Stir in honey and lemon juice.

7. Divide onion mixture evenly among bottoms of buns. Top each with one-quarter of the spinach and top of bun.

Makes 4 servings

MAKE AHEAD:
Prepare onion mixture, let cool, then cover and refrigerate for up to 3 or 4 days Microwave on high for 1-2 minutes to reheat before using.

The Monte Cristo

INGREDIENTS

- [ ] 2 thick slices white bread
- [ ] 1 tbsp (15 mL) mayonnaise
- [ ] 1 tsp (5 mL) Dijon mustard
- [ ] 1 egg
- [ ] ¼ cup (60 mL) milk
- [ ] Pinch each salt and pepper
- [ ] 3 slices (about 2 ½ oz/75 g) low-sodium ham
- [ ] 2 slices Swiss cheese

This sandwich combines all of the goodness of a gooey grilled cheese with salty ham in a French toast breading. Traditionalists serve it alongside a berry jam, but a steamy bowl of Roasted Red Pepper Soup (page 33) works nicely, too.

1. Spread 1 bread slice with mayonnaise, the other with mustard.

2. In shallow dish, whisk egg, milk, salt and pepper.

3. Dip first slice of bread into egg mixture. Transfer, mayonnaise-side up, to non-stick frying pan over medium heat.

4. Top with alternating slices of ham and cheese.

5. Dip remaining bread slice into egg mixture.

6. Place, mustard-side down, over sandwich fillings.

7. Cook sandwich until bottom is golden. With spatula, turn and cook until bottom is golden. Cut in half on diagonal.

Makes 1 serving

> **!**
> **TIP:**
> If cheese is slow to melt, reduce heat to medium-low, cover and cook, checking often to prevent burning.

FRENCH

Tomato, Basil & Mozza
GRILLED CHEESE

INGREDIENTS

- [ ] ¹/₂ to 1 beefsteak tomato, sliced
- [ ] 2 tsp (10 mL) balsamic vinegar
- [ ] ¹/₂ clove garlic, minced
- [ ] 1 tbsp (15 mL) olive oil
- [ ] 2 slices Italian bread
- [ ] 2 slices mozzarella cheese
- [ ] 4 or 5 basil leaves
- [ ] ¹/₈ tsp (0.5 mL) pepper

This sophisticated sandwich bursts with the flavours of an Italian summer. Try serving it with a green salad or alongside the Rustic Minestrone Soup (page 34).

1. In small bowl, cover tomato with vinegar; let marinate for 3 to 4 minutes.

2. In another small bowl, stir garlic with oil. Brush over 1 bread slice and transfer, oil-side down, to non-stick frying pan over medium-high heat.

3. Brush oil mixture on top. Top with cheese, basil, tomato mixture and pepper.

4. Brush oil mixture over 1 side of remaining bread slice. Place, oil-side down over sandwich filling.

5. Brush oil mixture on top.

6. Cook sandwich until bottom is golden brown and cheese is beginning to melt. With spatula, gently turn. Cook until bottom is golden brown. Cut in half on diagonal.

Makes 1 sandwich

VEGETARIAN

ITALIAN AMERICAN

TIP:
If cheese is slow to melt, reduce heat to medium-low, cover and cook, checking often to prevent burning.

Apple, Bacon & Gouda
Grilled Cheese

INGREDIENTS

- [ ] 4 slices bacon
- [ ] 4 slices sourdough bread
- [ ] 2 tsp (10 mL) Dijon mustard
- [ ] 1 Granny Smith apple
- [ ] 4 slices Gouda cheese

TIPS:

When frying bacon, always start with a cold pan. Evenly space slices in non-stick frying pan, then cook "low and slow" over medium to low heat, carefully spooning out excess fat as it accumulates, to avoid splattering.

If cheese is slow to melt, reduce heat to medium-low, cover and cook, checking often to prevent burning.

VARIATION:

If Granny Smith apples aren't available, other crisp, tart apples — such as Pink Lady, Gala and Honeycrisp — work well. Alternatively, try a Bartlett pear, or experiment with other seasonal fruit such as berries or peaches.

Crispy, gooey and incredibly flavourful, this sandwich is sure to please, either in small slices for an appetizer or snack, or eaten whole as a main meal with a simple green salad to round it out.

1. In non-stick frying pan over medium-low heat, cook the bacon low and slow (see TIP below), carefully spooning off excess grease as it accumulates into a separate grease jar so that it doesn't splatter.

2. While the bacon is frying, thinly slice apple, setting aside with cheese and bread.

3. Once the bacon has crisped to your liking, transfer it to a paper towel–lined plate.

4. Drain most of the bacon grease from the pan into a fat jar, reserving about 1 tablespoon and return to the stove, increasing the heat to medium.

5. Spread one side of 1 bread slice with half of the mustard; transfer, mustard-side up, to frying pan. Repeat with 1 bread slice and remaining mustard.

6. Top with half each of the apple, cheese and bacon and 1 remaining bread slice.

7. Cook sandwiches until bottoms are golden brown and cheese is beginning to melt.

8. With spatula, gently turn. Cook until bottoms are golden brown. Cut in half on diagonal.

Makes 2 sandwiches

DUTCH AMERICAN

Cheddar & Dill Pickle
GRILLED CHEESE

INGREDIENTS

- [ ] ½ tbsp (7 mL) butter, divided
- [ ] 2 slices sourdough or white bread
- [ ] 1 large dill pickle, sliced lengthwise
- [ ] 2 slices old cheddar cheese
- [ ] 2 tsp (10 mL) diced fresh dill

If dill isn't your thing, use bread-and-butter pickles, caramelized onions or even just slices of tomato. All these extras add swagger to the classic grilled cheese.

1. In non-stick frying pan over medium heat, melt half of the butter, place 1 bread slice in pan.

2. Top with pickle and cheese, then sprinkle evenly with dill. Top with remaining bread slice.

3. Cook sandwich until bottom is crisp and golden brown.

4. With spatula, lift sandwich. Melt remaining butter in pan. Turn sandwich over, return to pan.

5. Cook until bottom is crisp and golden brown. Cut in half on diagonal.

Makes 1 sandwich

VEGETARIAN

NORTH AMERICAN

TIP:
If cheese is slow to melt, reduce heat to medium-low, cover and cook, checking often to prevent burning.

Best Black Bean Burgers

INGREDIENTS

- [ ] 1 can (19 oz/540 mL) black beans, drained and rinsed
- [ ] 1 egg
- [ ] 2 cloves garlic, minced
- [ ] 1/2 small red onion, grated
- [ ] 1/2 cup (125 mL) bread crumbs
- [ ] 1 tbsp (15 mL) chili powder
- [ ] 1 tsp (5 mL) ground cumin
- [ ] 2 tbsp (30 mL) canola oil
- [ ] 2 slices cheddar cheese
- [ ] 2 hamburger buns, toasted
- [ ] 2 tbsp (30 mL) mayonnaise
- [ ] 2 large leaves lettuce
- [ ] 2 to 4 slices tomato
- [ ] 1 dill pickle, sliced lengthwise
- [ ] 1/2 tbsp (10 mL) store-bought hot sauce

An earthy black bean–based meal that even a carnivore would swoon over, this healthy alternative for a cheeseburger doesn't feel like even the slightest sacrifice.

1. In large bowl with potato masher, break up beans until some coarse crumbs remain.

2. Stir in egg, garlic, onion, bread crumbs, chili powder and cumin to combine and coat.

3. Let stand for 5 to 10 minutes.

4. With hands, form 2 firm patties, each about 1-inch (2.5 cm) thick.

5. In non-stick frying pan over medium-high heat, warm the oil. Cook patties for 5 minutes.

6. With spatula, turn patties. Top each with half of the cheese.

7. Cook until cheese is melted and bottom of patty is golden, about 4 to 5 minutes.

8. Spread bottom of each bun with half of the mayonnaise and top with patty. Top with half each of the lettuce, tomato, pickle, hot sauce and bun top.

Makes 2 burgers

MAKE AHEAD:
Prepare bean mixture, cover and refrigerate for up to 2 days before using.

VEGETARIAN

TEX-MEX

Crispy Tuna Burger

INGREDIENTS

- [ ] 1 can (6 oz/170 g) water-packed chunk or flaked tuna, drained
- [ ] 1/2 cup (125 mL) panko bread crumbs
- [ ] 1/4 cup (60 mL) celery, finely diced
- [ ] 1/4 cup (60 mL) onion, finely diced
- [ ] 1/2 tsp (2 mL) dried dill, crumbled
- [ ] 1 egg
- [ ] 1 tbsp (15 mL) mayonnaise
- [ ] 1 tbsp (15 mL) lemon juice
- [ ] 1 tsp (5 mL) hot pepper sauce
- [ ] 2 tbsp (30 mL) oil
- [ ] 2 slices cheddar cheese
- [ ] 2 hamburger buns, toasted

CABBAGE COLESLAW

- [ ] 2 tbsp (30 mL) mayonnaise
- [ ] 1 tbsp (15 mL) apple cider vinegar
- [ ] Salt and pepper to taste
- [ ] 1 carrot, grated
- [ ] 1 green onion, thinly sliced
- [ ] 1/2 apple, grated
- [ ] 1 cup (250 mL) shredded cabbage

TIP:
Non-reactive bowls are typically made from stainless steel, plastic or glass, materials that are not corroded by acidic or salty foods. "Reactive" bowls, such as those made of copper or aluminum, may react with these foods to impart a metallic taste to the food.

Like shellfish, light tuna contains a small amount of mercury, but is still safe to consume in modest quantities. Generally, the larger the fish, the more mercury it contains. Unlike tuna steaks, canned tuna is harvested from smaller fish and therefore contains less mercury. If protecting the oceans is important to you, try to purchase tuna that has been sustainably caught.

1. Coleslaw: In large non-reactive bowl (see TIP below), whisk mayonnaise, vinegar, salt and pepper. Toss in carrot, green onion, apple and cabbage to coat; set aside.

2. In bowl, toss together tuna, bread crumbs, celery, onion and dill.

3. In small bowl, whisk egg, mayonnaise, lemon juice and hot pepper sauce until blended and smooth. Pour over bread crumb mixture.

4. With hands, thoroughly combine, then form into 2 patties 1 inch (2.5 cm) in thickness.

5. In non-stick frying pan over medium-high heat, warm oil. Cook patties until bottoms are golden brown, about 4 to 5 minutes.

6. With spatula, turn patties and top each with half of the cheese. Cook until cheese has melted and bottoms are golden brown, about 4 minutes.

7. Top bottom of each bun with patty, cheese side up, then half of the coleslaw and top of bun.

Makes 2 burgers

VARIATION:
For a "lighter" burger, omit the cheese and use large lettuce leaves as the "buns."

MAKE AHEAD:
Assemble the patties, then cover with plastic wrap and refrigerate for up to 24 hours before cooking.

NORTH AMERICAN

Baked Falafel Pita
w/ Cucumber Dressing

INGREDIENTS

FALAFELS

- [ ] 3 cloves garlic
- [ ] ¹/₂ small yellow onion, chopped
- [ ] ¹/₄ cup (60 mL) fresh cilantro leaves, chopped
- [ ] 2 tbsp (30 mL) lemon juice
- [ ] 1 tsp (5 mL) salt
- [ ] 1 can (14 oz/398 mL) chickpeas, rinsed and drained
- [ ] 2 tbsp (30 mL) all-purpose flour
- [ ] 2 tbsp (30 mL) olive oil
- [ ] 1 tsp (5 mL) crumbled dried oregano
- [ ] 3 small pitas, warmed (see TIP below)
- [ ] 4 or 5 leaves romaine lettuce, chopped
- [ ] 1 tomato, chopped
- [ ] ¹/₄ red onion, sliced

CUCUMBER DRESSING

- [ ] 1 small garlic clove, minced
- [ ] ¹/₂ cup (125 mL) chopped cucumber
- [ ] 1 tbsp (15 mL) olive oil
- [ ] 1 tsp (5 mL) crumbled dried dill
- [ ] ¹/₂ cup (125 mL) plain Greek yogurt
- [ ] 1 tsp (5 mL) lemon juice

Preparing these little lemony, garlicky chickpea patties is a snap, because they're baked instead of fried. Tuck one inside a warmed pita with veggies and tart yogurt dressing for a quick snack or a light meal.

1. Preheat oven to 425°F (220°C).

2. In food processor or blender, pulse together garlic, onion, cilantro, lemon juice and salt until diced.

3. Add half the chickpeas and pulse until coarsely blended.

4. Transfer to bowl. With fork, mash in remaining chickpeas. Stir in flour, oil and oregano.

5. With hands, form 9 patties, each about 1/2-inch (~1 cm) thick.

6. Transfer to parchment paper–lined rimmed baking sheet.

7. Bake in oven, turning once halfway through, until golden brown and crisp, about 20 minutes.

8. Dressing: Meanwhile, in food processor or blender, purée garlic, cucumber, oil and dill until blended and smooth. Stir in yogurt and lemon juice until blended.

9. Open each pita and stuff with one-third each of the lettuce, tomato and onion, and a patty. Drizzle dressing over filling in each pita and wrap tightly.

Makes 3 pitas

VEGETARIAN

MIDDLE EASTERN

TIP:
To warm each pita, microwave for 10 to 15 seconds.

MAKE AHEAD:
Separately cover and refrigerate dressing and leftover pitas for up to 3 to 4 days, then combine for quick sandwiches.

BLT with Avocado

INGREDIENTS

- [ ] 6 slices (approx 1 1/2 oz/45 g) bacon
- [ ] 4 leaves lettuce
- [ ] 1 beefsteak tomato
- [ ] 4 slices sourdough bread
- [ ] 1/2 avocado, peeled, pitted and sliced
- [ ] 1 tbsp (15 mL) lemon juice
- [ ] 2 tbsp (30 mL) light mayonnaise
- [ ] 2 tsp (10 mL) Sriracha hot sauce (optional)

Almost anything can be improved by adding avocado, including the classic BLT. Creamy avocado enhances crispy bacon on top of a bed of lettuce, tomato and sourdough. Serve with optional hot sauce mixed into the mayonnaise for those who like life a little spicier.

1. When frying bacon, always start with a cold pan. Lay the slices in a non-stick frying pan, evenly spaced and turn to a medium-low heat. Cook the bacon low and slow, carefully spooning off excess grease as it accumulates into a separate grease jar so that it doesn't splatter.

2. While the bacon is frying, wash and dry the lettuce and slice the tomato, setting it aside with the bread. Slice the avocado and pour lemon juice over top so that it doesn't brown.

3. Once the bacon has crisped to your liking, transfer it to a paper towel–lined plate.

4. Toast the bread and spread with roughly half the mayonnaise. Assemble the sandwich with half of the sliced avocado, bacon, tomato and lettuce and the other slice of bread.

5. Remove from the pan and repeat the process with remaining ingredients for the second sandwich. Slice diagonally to serve.

Makes 2 sandwiches

NORTH AMERICAN

Bahn Mi
MEATBALL SUB

INGREDIENTS

- [ ] 1 lb (450 g) extra-lean ground chicken or pork
- [ ] 3 cloves garlic
- [ ] 1 tbsp (15 mL) fish sauce
- [ ] 1 tsp (5 mL) Sriracha sauce
- [ ] 1 tbsp (15 mL) brown sugar
- [ ] 1/2 cup (125 mL) mayonnaise
- [ ] 1 tbsp (15 mL) Sriracha sauce
- [ ] 1 baguette cut into 4 sections or 4 crusty sandwich buns

COLESLAW

- [ ] 1/4 cup (60 mL) rice vinegar
- [ ] 2 tbsp (30 mL) honey
- [ ] 1 tbsp (15 mL) toasted sesame oil
- [ ] 1 cups (250 mL) cabbage, grated
- [ ] 1/2 cup (125 mL) carrot, grated
- [ ] 1/2 cup (125 mL) cucumber, thinly sliced
- [ ] 1/2 cup (125 mL) red onion, thinly sliced
- [ ] 1/2 cup (125 mL) cup fresh cilantro, chopped

The bahn mi is a fusion of French and Vietnamese cuisine. The classic baguette combined with the sweet, sour and spicy meats characteristic of the Vietnamese cooking is complemented nicely with the crunch of vegetables.

1. In a large mixing bowl, use your hands to combine the meat, garlic, fish sauce, first amount Sriracha and brown sugar. Mix well and allow it to marinate at room temperature for 30 minutes or in the fridge for a couple hours. Roll out into meatballs, roughly 1 tbsp (15 mL) sized, and place on a plate.

2. Stir together the mayonnaise and second amount Sriracha and refrigerate to reserve.

3. Preheat a non-stick pan over medium heat.

4. Place the meatballs in the pan to fry for 10 to 15 minutes, shaking the pan to roll them around every 3 minutes or so. Ensure that the meatballs are cooked through before removing them from the heat.

5. While the meatballs fry, assemble the coleslaw by whisking together the rice vinegar, honey and sesame oil in a large bowl. Add the cabbage, carrot, cucumber, onion, and cilantro and toss to coat.

6. Spread each side of the sandwich bun with the spicy mayo and distribute the coleslaw among them. Top with the meatballs and enjoy.

Makes 4 subs

ASIAN (VIETNAMESE)

Kofta Burgers
& YOGURT SAUCE

INGREDIENTS

- [ ] 1 lb (500 g) extra-lean ground beef
- [ ] 4 cloves garlic, minced
- [ ] 2 tbsp (30 mL) garam masala
- [ ] 1/2 cup (125 mL) cilantro, chopped
- [ ] Pinch crushed red pepper
- [ ] 1 cup (250 mL) Greek yogurt
- [ ] 1 small chili pepper, minced
- [ ] 1 clove garlic, minced
- [ ] 4 pitas
- [ ] 2 cups (500 mL) red cabbage, shredded
- [ ] 1 large tomato, sliced
- [ ] 1/2 small red onion, thinly sliced

Kofta is a super-spiced ground meat patty of Middle Eastern origin. These burgers fit perfectly into a pita with classic red onion, tomato and yogurt sauce.

1. In large mixing bowl, use your hands to combine the meat, garlic, garam masala, cilantro and crushed red pepper. Mix well and allow it to marinate at room temperature for 30 minutes or in the fridge for a couple hours. Roll out into roughly 8 patties, 1/4 cup (60 mL) sized.

2. Meanwhile, stir together the yogurt, chili pepper and clove of garlic and refrigerate to reserve.

3. Preheat oven to 200°F (90°C) and line a baking sheet with parchment paper.

4. Once meat has marinated, heat a non-stick frying pan over medium-high heat. Fry each patty until cooked through and reserve the cooked patties inside the warm oven.

5. Assemble the burgers by lining the pitas with the cabbage, tomato and onion. Top with a dollop of the yogurt sauce and 2 kofta patties.

Makes 4 burgers

MIDDLE EASTERN

The Main Deal

Vegetable FRIED QUINOA

INGREDIENTS

- ☐ 2 tbsp (30 mL) butter, divided
- ☐ 1 yellow onion, thinly sliced
- ☐ 4 cloves garlic, minced or pressed
- ☐ 1-inch (2.5 cm) piece fresh ginger, minced
- ☐ 1 carrot, thinly sliced on diagonal
- ☐ ¹/₂ cup (125 mL) button mushrooms, thinly sliced
- ☐ ¹/₂ cup (125 mL) drained canned or thawed frozen baby peas
- ☐ ¹/₂ cup (125 mL) drained canned or thawed frozen corn kernels
- ☐ 2 cups (500 mL) cooked quinoa, cooled
- ☐ 2 eggs, beaten
- ☐ 2 tbsp (30 mL) soy sauce
- ☐ 1 tbsp (15 mL) sesame oil
- ☐ Store-bought hot sauce (optional)

This is a 'kitchen sink" recipe, where just about anything goes. Using up leftovers is a great way to stretch your food budget and ensure nothing goes to waste. Try adding your favourite veggies, and pair this with a side of protein to make a complete meal.

1. In large frying pan over medium-high heat, melt 1 tbsp (15 mL) of the butter; sauté onion until golden brown, about 10 minutes.

2. Stir in garlic and ginger; sauté for 2 to 3 minutes. Toss in carrot, mushrooms, peas and corn; sauté for 3 to 4 minutes.

3. Transfer to bowl; cover and keep warm.

4. In pan, melt remaining butter; stir in quinoa and cook, stirring, until heated through. With spatula, stir in eggs until combined; stir in onion mixture, soy sauce and oil until combined. Garnish with hot sauce (if using).

Makes 2 servings

VARIATION:
To make this recipe vegan, omit the eggs, and replace the butter with an equal amount of 2 tbsp (30 mL) canola oil.

VEGETARIAN

VEGAN

ASIAN

shrimp & vegetable
FRIED RICE

INGREDIENTS

- [ ] 2 tbsp (30 mL) butter, divided
- [ ] 1 yellow onion, thinly sliced
- [ ] ¹/₂ lb (225 g) shrimp, peeled, deveined and chopped
- [ ] 4 cloves garlic, minced or pressed
- [ ] 1-inch (2.5 cm) piece fresh ginger, minced
- [ ] 1 carrot, thinly sliced on diagonal
- [ ] ¹/₂ cup (125 mL) broccoli, finely chopped
- [ ] ¹/₂ cup (125 mL) fresh or thawed frozen peas
- [ ] ¹/₂ cup (125 mL) drained canned or thawed frozen corn kernels
- [ ] 2 cups (500 mL) cooled cooked brown rice
- [ ] 1 egg, beaten
- [ ] 2 tbsp (30 mL) soy sauce
- [ ] 1 tbsp (15 mL) sesame oil
- [ ] Hot sauce (optional)

Easy to make ahead, this leftover takeout rice tastes even better the second time around. Try substituting equal amounts of thawed from frozen cooked shrimp instead of raw and thawed mixed vegetables to make this recipe a cinch. Stir-frying uses minimal oil and a high heat to quickly cook the vegetables and keeps that satisfying 'bite" or crunch.

1. In large frying pan over high heat, melt 1 tbsp (15 mL) of the butter; sauté onion until golden brown, about 5 minutes, stirring constantly and being careful not to burn.

2. Stir in shrimp, garlic and ginger; sauté until shrimp is pink all over, 1 to 2 minutes.

3. With slotted spoon, transfer to bowl; cover and keep warm.

4. In pan, stir-fry carrot, broccoli, peas and corn just until tender, 3 to 4 minutes; with slotted spoon transfer to bowl; cover and keep warm. In pan, melt remaining butter; with spatula, spread rice in pan and cook, stirring to coat, until heated through, 1 to 2 minutes. With spatula, stir in egg until combined. Stir in onion and shrimp mixture, carrot mixture, soy sauce and oil until combined. Serve with hot sauce (if using) on side.

Makes 2 servings

ASIAN

 TIP:
If you're planning to use leftover rice in this dish, remember that rice can be refrigerated for only 4 days at most. After that, it's best to discard it to minimize your risk of food-borne illness.

'Anytime' Tofu
PAD THAI

INGREDIENTS

- [ ] 1 package (6 oz/170 g) Thai rice noodles
- [ ] 3 tbsp (45 mL) sesame oil, divided
- [ ] 2 eggs, beaten
- [ ] 3 oz (85 g) tofu, pressed (see TIPS on next page) and cut into roughly ½ inch (1.25 cm) cubes
- [ ] ¼ cup (60 mL) shallots, chopped
- [ ] 2 green onions, thinly sliced on diagonal
- [ ] 1 carrot, thinly sliced on diagonal
- [ ] ½ sweet red pepper, thinly sliced
- [ ] 2 cups (500 mL) fresh bean sprouts
- [ ] ¼ cup (60 mL) fresh cilantro, chopped
- [ ] ¼ cup (60 mL) salted peanuts, chopped
- [ ] ½ lime, in wedges

SAUCE

- [ ] 2 tbsp (30 mL) lime juice
- [ ] 1 tbsp (15 mL) packed brown sugar
- [ ] 1 tbsp (15 mL) sesame oil
- [ ] 1 tbsp (15 mL) Sriracha hot sauce
- [ ] 1 tbsp (15 mL) fish sauce
- [ ] 1 tbsp (15 mL) rice vinegar
- [ ] 1 tbsp (15 mL) soy sauce

Sweet, spicy, sour noodles — this version of the Thai favourite is healthy enough to be eaten any time and easy enough to make at home. Chicken and shrimp make excellent additions to this dish.

1. In large bowl, cover noodles with hot water from the tap; let stand until softened, 3 to 4 minutes. Drain, rinse and return to dry bowl.

2. Toss in 1 tbsp (15 mL) of the oil to coat; set aside.

3. Sauce: In small bowl, whisk lime juice, brown sugar, oil, Sriracha sauce, fish sauce, vinegar and soy sauce until blended and smooth; set aside.

4. In large non-stick frying pan over medium-high heat, swirl eggs to coat bottom; cook, without stirring, until set.

5. With spatula, flip entire egg 'patty" and cook for 30 to 60 seconds; slip onto plate and let cool.

6. Roll up egg 'patty," then slice into thin ribbons; transfer to bowl with noodles.

7. In pan, warm 1 tbsp (15 mL) of the oil; sauté tofu until golden brown, about 5 minutes.

8. Transfer to the bowl with noodles.

9. In pan, warm remaining oil; sauté shallots until tender, about 3 to 4 minutes.

10. Toss in noodle mixture, onions, carrot, red pepper, bean sprouts and cilantro to combine.

11. Toss in sauce to coat.

12. Transfer to 2 serving bowls; garnish with peanuts. Serve with lime on side.

Makes 2 servings

TIPS:
Pressing tofu removes moisture, making the tofu chewier and better able to absorb flavours and sauce. Here's how: Lay several thicknesses of paper towel over a small plate, centering tofu block on top. Lay several thicknesses of paper towel over tofu; top with cookbooks and cans and let stand for at least 15 minutes.
If shallots are not available or too costly, substitute with equal amount (1/4 cup/ 60 mL) diced white onion and two minced cloves garlic.

simple sesame
CHICKEN

INGREDIENTS

- ☐ 1 egg
- ☐ 2 tbsp (30 mL) cornstarch
- ☐ ¹/₄ tsp (1 mL) black pepper
- ☐ 1 lb (450 g) boneless skinless chicken thighs, fat trimmed, cut in bite-size pieces
- ☐ 1 tbsp (15 mL) canola oil
- ☐ 1 clove garlic, minced
- ☐ Sliced green onion and/or fresh cilantro leaves, for garnish

SAUCE

- ☐ 1-inch (2.5 cm) piece fresh ginger, minced or grated
- ☐ 2 tbsp (30 mL) packed brown sugar
- ☐ 2 tbsp (30 mL) sesame seeds
- ☐ 2 tbsp (30 mL) rice vinegar
- ☐ 2 tbsp (30 mL) soy sauce
- ☐ 1 tbsp (15 mL) cornstarch
- ☐ 1 tbsp (15 mL) water
- ☐ ¹/₂ tbsp (7 mL) toasted sesame oil

A favourite Chinese-takeout treat, this version takes less time than the delivery and costs a fraction of the price. Spicy Sriracha, nutty sesame, salty soy and sweet brown sugar makes one of the cheaper cuts of meat ultra-satisfying. Try spooning this recipe over steamed rice, wrapped with crisp iceberg lettuce leaves or spooned over stir-fried veggies.

1. In large bowl, whisk egg, cornstarch and pepper until blended; toss in chicken to coat.

2. In non-stick frying pan over medium-high heat, warm oil with garlic; sauté chicken until slightly crisp, golden brown and cooked through, about 4 to 5 minutes.

3. Sauce: In bowl, whisk ginger, brown sugar, sesame seeds, vinegar, soy sauce, cornstarch, water and oil until blended and smooth.

4. Stir into chicken to coat and cook until sauce is thickened and gelled, about 5 minutes.

5. Transfer to serving dish; garnish with green onion and/or cilantro.

Makes 4 servings

VARIATION:
Try using a 14-oz block of cubed extra-firm tofu instead of chicken for a vegetarian alternative.

ASIAN

Hoisin Chicken
Lettuce Wraps

INGREDIENTS

- [ ] 1 tbsp (15 mL) canola oil
- [ ] 1 yellow onion, diced
- [ ] 4 cloves garlic, minced or pressed
- [ ] 1 lb (450 g) lean ground chicken
- [ ] 1 can (8 oz/228 g) can water chestnuts, drained and chopped
- [ ] 1/2 sweet red pepper, thinly sliced
- [ ] 1/2 tbsp (7 mL) sesame oil
- [ ] 12 large outer leaves lettuce
- [ ] 2 green onions, thinly sliced on diagonal

SAUCE

- [ ] 1-inch (2.5 cm) piece fresh ginger, minced
- [ ] 1/4 cup (60 mL) hoisin sauce
- [ ] 2 tbsp (30 mL) soy sauce
- [ ] 1 tbsp (15 mL) rice vinegar
- [ ] 1/2 tbsp (7 mL) Sriracha sauce

Using a vegetable as the vehicle to get the good stuff to your mouth is nothing short of genius. These Asian-inspired 'tacos" may leave you wrapping all your meals in lettuce from here on, and that's far from a bad thing.

1. Sauce: In small bowl, whisk ginger, hoisin sauce, soy sauce, vinegar and Sriracha sauce until blended and smooth; set aside.

2. In large frying pan over medium-high heat, warm canola oil. Sauté onion until golden brown, about 4 minutes. Stir in garlic; sauté for 1 to 2 minutes.

3. Stir in chicken; sauté, breaking up with spatula, until browned and cooked through, about 6 to 8 minutes.

4. Stir in sauce, water chestnuts and red pepper; sauté for 1 to 2 minutes.

5. Stir in sesame oil.

6. Divide mixture evenly among lettuce leaves; sprinkle with green onions. To eat, simply fold or roll the goodness inside the leaf just as you would a taco or burrito.

Makes 4 servings

ASIAN (CHINESE)

VARIATION:
To make this recipe vegan, use 1 1/3 cups (315 mL) textured vegetable protein (TVP)

TIP:
TVP is an excellent meat extender or substitute in virtually any recipe. Because it consists of de-fatted soy protein, it has all the benefits of protein and fibre without any calories from fat. Try rehydrated in (1 cup) vegetable stock or crumbled thawed from frozen tofu.

Cashew Chicken

INGREDIENTS

- [ ] 1 lb (450 g) boneless skinless chicken thighs, cubed
- [ ] ¹/₄ tsp (1 mL) salt
- [ ] ¹/₈ tsp (0.5 mL) pepper
- [ ] 1 tbsp (15 mL) vegetable oil
- [ ] 4 garlic cloves, minced
- [ ] 1-inch (2.5 cm) piece fresh ginger, minced
- [ ] ³/₄ cup (175 mL) chopped onion
- [ ] ¹/₂ tsp (2 mL) red pepper flakes
- [ ] ¹/₂ cup (125 mL) toasted cashews

SAUCE

- [ ] ¹/₂ cup (125 mL) chicken broth
- [ ] 1¹/₂ tbsp (22 mL) soy sauce
- [ ] 1 ¹/₂ tsp (7 mL) cornstarch
- [ ] 1 tsp (5 mL) sugar

ASIAN (CHINESE)

A great way to use chicken thighs you've bought on sale is to batch-cook this delicious dish, then freeze single-serve portions for an easy evening meal after a long day. This recipe will have you waving goodbye to expensive takeout. Serve over a steaming bowl of brown or basmati rice to soak up the sauce.

1. Sauce: In bowl, whisk chicken broth, soy sauce, cornstarch and sugar until blended and smooth; set aside.

2. With paper towel, pat chicken dry. Sprinkle with salt and pepper. Set aside.

3. In non-stick frying pan over high heat, warm oil. Stir-fry chicken until golden brown and cooked through, about 4 to 5 minutes, and transfer to plate.

4. In pan, sauté garlic, ginger, onion and red pepper flakes just until onion is tender, about 3 to 4 minutes.

5. Stir in sauce; reduce heat and simmer, stirring occasionally, until sauce is thickened and gelled, about 3 to 4 minutes.

6. Gently toss in chicken and cashews until coated and heated through.

Makes 2 servings

VARIATION:
If cashews are too pricey, less-expensive almonds or peanuts also work well.

MAKE AHEAD:
Separately mix sauce and cook chicken; cover and refrigerate individually for up to 4 days. Stir-fry vegetables, then toss in chicken, cashews and sauce until heated through.

Easy Szechuan Tofu
Carrots, Peppers & Broccoli

INGREDIENTS

SAUCE

- ☐ 3 tbsp (45 mL) low-sodium vegetable stock
- ☐ 1 tbsp (15 mL) tomato paste
- ☐ 1 tbsp (15 mL) rice vinegar
- ☐ 1 tsp (5 mL) sugar
- ☐ 1 tsp (5 mL) cornstarch
- ☐ 1 tsp (5 mL) Sriracha sauce (or ½ tsp/2 mL red pepper flakes)
- ☐ ½ tbsp (7 mL) low-sodium soy sauce

STIR-FRY

- ☐ 1½ cups (375 mL) cooked rice, cooled
- ☐ 2 tbsp (30 mL) canola oil, divided
- ☐ 14 oz (400 g) block firm tofu, pressed (see TIP on page 90) and cubed
- ☐ 2 green onions, thinly sliced on diagonal
- ☐ 2 cloves garlic, minced
- ☐ 1-inch (2.5 cm) piece fresh ginger, grated
- ☐ 2 cups (500 mL) fresh or thawed frozen broccoli florets, chopped
- ☐ 2 carrots, thinly sliced on diagonal
- ☐ 1 sweet pepper, chopped
- ☐ ½ tbsp (7 mL) toasted sesame oil

This is a twist on the authentic 'ma po dou fu" (translated: pock-marked old woman) dish originating from the Szechuan province of China. As the story goes, a woman with pock-marked skin created this spicy and savoury dish to welcome visitors to her husband's restaurant in that region. Not entirely authentic, this version is a tasty, easy and fast approximation best served with a big heap of rice.

1. Sauce: In large bowl, whisk vegetable stock, tomato paste, vinegar, sugar, cornstarch, Sriracha sauce and soy sauce until blended and smooth. Set aside.

2. In large saucepan over high heat, warm 1 tbsp (15 mL) of the canola oil. Fry tofu and onions, stirring once halfway through, until tofu edges are crisp, about 5 to 6 minutes.

3. Stir into sauce. Let stand for a couple of minutes to marinate while you stir-fry the vegetables next.

4. In pan, stir-fry garlic, ginger and broccoli until broccoli is bright green, 1 to 2 minutes.

5. Toss in carrots and sweet pepper; stir-fry for 1 to 2 minutes.

6. Gently scrape in sauce mixture; stir-fry until heated through and sauce is thickened, about 2 to 3 minutes.

7. Stir in sesame oil.

Makes 4 servings

VARIATION:
Add 1 lb (450 g) thinly sliced pork or extra lean ground chicken in addition to or instead of tofu for a meaty alternative.

VEGETARIAN

VEGAN

ASIAN (CHINESE)

sticky & sweet Tofu
STEAKS WITH ASPARAGUS

INGREDIENTS

- ☐ ¹/₄ cup (60 mL) all-purpose flour
- ☐ ¹/₂ tsp (2 mL) salt
- ☐ ¹/₂ tsp (2 mL) pepper
- ☐ 14 oz (400 g) block firm tofu, pressed (see TIP on page 90) and sliced in 8 rectangles
- ☐ 2 tbsp (30 mL) coconut oil, divided
- ☐ 1 bunch (1 lb/450 g) asparagus, trimmed
- ☐ 2 green onions, thinly sliced on diagonal, white and green parts separated
- ☐ 1 tbsp (15 mL) toasted sesame seeds (optional)
- ☐ 1¹/₂ cups (375 mL) brown rice, cooked

SAUCE

- ☐ 1 tbsp (15 mL) liquid honey
- ☐ ¹/₂ tsp (8 mL) low-sodium soy sauce
- ☐ 1 tsp (5 mL) Sriracha sauce

Asparagus is one of those vegetables that might have been ruined for you as a kid — served soggy, brown and boiled to a pulp. Now that you've grown up, give it a second chance in this sweet and savoury Asian-inspired recipe. Snap off the woody ends of the spears, then fry them until they're bright and tender-crisp.

1. Sauce: In small bowl, whisk honey, soy sauce and Sriracha sauce; set aside.

2. In small bowl, whisk flour, salt and pepper. One piece at a time, dip tofu into flour mixture, turning to coat all over; transfer to plate and set aside.

3. In large saucepan or wok, melt 1 tbsp (15 mL) of the oil over high heat. Stir-fry asparagus until bright green and tender-crisp, about 3 minutes.

4. With tongs, transfer to serving plate. Set aside and keep warm.

5. In pan, melt remaining oil. Sauté tofu and white parts of green onions until golden and crisp, about 6 to 8 minutes.

6. With slotted spoon, transfer to plate with asparagus. Drizzle with sauce; sprinkle with green parts of green onions and sesame seeds (if using). Serve with rice.

Makes 4 servings

VEGETARIAN

VEGAN

ASIAN

VARIATION:
For a meaty alternative, use 1 lb (450 g) thinly sliced pork or beef instead of tofu.

Broccoli Pad See Ew

INGREDIENTS

SAUCE

- ☐ 2 tbsp (30 mL) oyster sauce
- ☐ 2 tbsp (30 mL) water
- ☐ 1 1/2 tbsp soy sauce
- ☐ 1 tbsp (15 mL) liquid honey
- ☐ 2 tsp (10 mL) vinegar

NOODLES

- ☐ 2 tbsp (30 mL) vegetable oil
- ☐ 2 cloves garlic
- ☐ 1 lb (450 g) boneless skinless chicken thighs, sliced
- ☐ 1 egg
- ☐ 2 cups (500 mL) broccoli, chopped, florets and tough stems separated
- ☐ 1 package (8 oz/225 g) pad thai or egg noodles, cooked, drained and cooled
- ☐ 2 green onions, thinly sliced on diagonal
- ☐ 1/2 tbsp (7 mL) toasted sesame seeds (optional)

Chewy rice noodles contrast with crunchy broccoli in a savoury-sweet gravy, to make this popular Thai street food a real winner. This dish is simple to make; instead of using a traditional dark soy sauce (which is thicker and sweeter than the regular stuff, but hard to find), we're sweetening common soy sauce with a bit of honey.

1. Sauce: In small bowl, whisk together oyster sauce, water, soy sauce, honey and vinegar; set aside.

2. In a frying pan over high heat, warm oil. Sauté garlic until golden.

3. Stir in chicken and broccoli stems. Sauté until chicken is golden, crisp and cooked through, then push chicken to edge of pan.

4. Carefully crack egg into centre of pan; with spatula, scramble.

5. Toss in broccoli florets, noodles and sauce; stir-fry to coat.

6. Transfer to serving plate; sprinkle with green onions and sesame seeds (if using).

Makes 4 servings

VARIATION:
For a vegan version, replace the chicken with 14 oz (400 g) crumbled thawed from frozen tofu.

ASIAN (CHINESE)

peanut Tofu
WITH CABBAGE & PEPPERS

INGREDIENTS

SAUCE

- ☐ 2 cloves garlic, minced
- ☐ 1-inch (2.5 cm) piece fresh ginger, minced
- ☐ 1/2 cup (125 mL) natural peanut butter
- ☐ 2 tbsp (30 mL) reduced-sodium soy sauce
- ☐ 1 tbsp (15 mL) lime juice
- ☐ 2 tsp (10 mL) packed brown sugar or honey
- ☐ 1 tsp (5 mL) Sriracha sauce or 1/2 tsp (2 mL) red pepper flakes

STIR-FRY

- ☐ 2 tbsp (30 mL) canola oil, divided
- ☐ 14 oz (400 g) block firm tofu, pressed (see TIP below) and cubed
- ☐ 1/2 yellow onion, sliced
- ☐ 4 cups (1 L) finely chopped cabbage
- ☐ 1 sweet pepper, chopped
- ☐ 1 1/2 cups (375 mL) white rice, cooked
- ☐ 2 tbsp (30 mL) fresh cilantro, chopped

Cabbage, peppers and tofu combine in a spicy, salty peanut sauce that is nothing less than addictive. This recipe is so incredibly inexpensive to make, you'll want to invite a crowd to enjoy this dish.

1. Sauce: In large bowl, whisk garlic, ginger, peanut butter, soy sauce, lime juice, brown sugar and Sriracha sauce until blended and smooth; set aside.

2. In large saucepan or wok over high heat, warm 1 tbsp (15 mL) of the oil. Sauté tofu until golden and crisp.

3. With slotted spoon, transfer to sauce. Let stand for a few minutes to marinate while you work on the vegetables.

4. In pan, warm remaining oil. Stir-fry onion, cabbage and sweet pepper just until cabbage is wilted, 1 to 2 minutes.

5. Stir in sauce mixture; cook, stirring, until heated through.

6. Transfer to serving dish over rice; garnish with cilantro.

Makes 4 servings

> **!**
>
> **TIP:**
> Pressing tofu makes the texture a bit chewier by lowering the water content. To do this easily, set the block of tofu on a paper towel lined plate, fold more paper towel to set on top and weigh it down with heavy books or cans for about 15 minutes.
>
> **VARIATION:**
> Try using 1 lb (450 g) thin slices or ground pork instead of tofu for a meaty alternative.

VEGETARIAN

VEGAN

ASIAN (THAI)

Tofu & vegetable
STIR-FRY IN PEANUT SAUCE

INGREDIENTS

SAUCE

- [ ] ¹/₂ cup (125 mL) peanut butter
- [ ] ¹/₂ cup (125 mL) hot water
- [ ] 2 tbsp (30 mL) reduced-sodium soy sauce
- [ ] 2 tbsp (30 mL) packed brown sugar
- [ ] 2 tbsp (30 mL) apple cider vinegar
- [ ] 1 tsp (5 mL) Sriracha sauce (or ¹/₂ tsp/2 mL chili paste)

STIR-FRY

- [ ] 1 tbsp (15 mL) canola oil
- [ ] 14 oz (400 g) block firm tofu, pressed (see TIP below) and cubed
- [ ] 1 head broccoli, chopped in florets
- [ ] 1 sweet red pepper, chopped
- [ ] 1 cup (250 mL) sugar snap peas, chopped

This vegan meal is super healthy and fast — not to mention delicious! Serve it over a steaming bowl of quinoa, rice or pasta.

1. Sauce: In small bowl, whisk peanut butter, water, soy sauce, brown sugar, vinegar and Sriracha sauce until blended and smooth. Set aside.

2. In large saucepan or wok over high heat, warm oil. Stir-fry tofu and broccoli for 1 to 2 minutes.

3. Stir in red pepper and peas. Stir-fry for about 1 minute.

4. Stir in sauce to coat. Simmer, stirring, until vegetables are tender-crisp and sauce is heated through, about 3 minutes.

Makes 4 servings

TIP:
Pressing tofu makes the texture a bit chewier by lowering the water content. To do this easily, set the block of tofu on a paper towel lined plate, fold more paper towel to set on top and weigh it down with heavy books or cans for about 15 minutes.

VARIATION:
For a meaty alternative, use 1 lb (450 g) thinly sliced chicken breast or pork instead of the tofu.

VEGETARIAN

VEGAN

ASIAN (THAI)

filipino pancit

VEGETARIAN

VEGAN

ASIAN (PHILIPPINE)

INGREDIENTS

- [ ] 6 oz (170 g) rice vermicelli
- [ ] 1 tsp (5 mL) sesame oil
- [ ] 2 tbsp (30 mL) coconut oil
- [ ] 2 cloves garlic, minced
- [ ] 1 small yellow onion, diced
- [ ] ¹/₄ lb (115 g) flank steak, thinly sliced against the grain
- [ ] 3 carrots, thinly sliced
- [ ] ¹/₂ small head green cabbage, thinly sliced
- [ ] 3 tbsp (45 mL) soy sauce
- [ ] ¹/₂ lemon, quartered in wedges

Pancit (pronounced 'pan-sit") is a staple street food of the Philippines consisting of noodles (introduced to their culture by the Chinese) stir-fried with cabbage and less-common cuts of meat. Unlike their similar Chinese versions, Philipine noodle dishes often use coconut oil and citrus juices, adding a tropical taste twist. Commonly served on birthdays, the unbroken noodles in this dish symbolize a long and prosperous life.

1. In large bowl, cover vermicelli with warm water. Let soak until softened, about 3 minutes.

2. Drain, rinse and transfer to dry bowl.

3. Toss in sesame oil to coat and prevent the noodles from sticking together and set aside.

4. In non-stick frying pan, warm oil. Sauté garlic and onion just until onion is translucent.

5. Stir in steak, carrots and cabbage. Stir-fry until vegetables are softened, about 3 minutes.

6. Toss in soy sauce and noodles to coat. Serve with lemon wedges.

Makes 2 servings

> **VARIATION:**
> For a vegan alternative, substitute ¹/₂ cup (125 mL) diced tofu for the steak.

Thai Chicken,
Vegetable & Peanut Sauce Noodles

INGREDIENTS

- ☐ 4 oz (115 g) whole-grain spaghetti (³/₄ inch diameter) or 4 oz/115 g Thai-style rice noodles, cooked, drained and cooled
- ☐ 1 tbsp (15 mL) canola or coconut oil
- ☐ 1 clove garlic, minced
- ☐ ¹/₂-inch (1 cm) piece fresh ginger, grated
- ☐ ¹/₂ lb (225 g) lean ground chicken
- ☐ ¹/₂ cup (125 mL) low-sodium chicken or vegetable stock
- ☐ 2 carrots, thinly sliced or julienned
- ☐ 1 sweet red pepper, thinly sliced
- ☐ 3 green onions, thinly sliced
- ☐ ¹/₄ cup (60 mL) fresh cilantro leaves
- ☐ ¹/₄ cup (60 mL) salted roasted peanut pieces (optional)

SAUCE

- ☐ ¹/₄ cup (60 mL) natural creamy peanut butter
- ☐ ¹/₄ cup (60 mL) lime juice
- ☐ 2 tbsp (30 mL) packed brown sugar
- ☐ 2 tbsp (30 mL) low-sodium soy sauce
- ☐ 2 tsp (10 mL) Asian chili paste or hot sauce

The ultimate exotic comfort food looks exactly like this: creamy peanut butter, salty soy, sweet and spicy chilies, and steamy, carb-rich pasta. This dish is super-easy, cheap and a real crowd-pleaser. Try serving it with extra chili sauce on the table so brave folks can bump up the heat.

1. Sauce: In small bowl, whisk peanut butter, lime juice, brown sugar, soy sauce and chili paste until blended and smooth. Set aside.

2. In large frying pan over medium-high heat, warm oil. Sauté garlic and ginger for 15 to 30 seconds.

3. Stir in chicken, breaking up with spoon.

4. Stir in stock and carrots. Cook, stirring, until chicken is cooked through and the stock is reduced by about half, 6 to 8 minutes.

5. Stir in sauce; toss in red pepper and noodles to coat.

6. Cook, stirring, until heated through.

7. Transfer to serving plate; garnish with green onions, cilantro, and peanuts (if using).

Makes 2 servings

VARIATION:
You can substitute equal amounts of other leftover thinly-sliced meat or vegan/vegetarian protein sources (such as cubed tofu or edamame beans) for the ground chicken.

MAKE AHEAD:
Separately cook ground chicken, cover and refrigerate; prepare, cover and refrigerate sauce, vegetables and noodles, all for up to 2 to 3 days. In screaming-hot wok, toss together with 1 tbsp (15 mL) oil; stir-fry until heated through, 2 minutes or less.

carrots, sesame
& Soy Ramen 'takeout' Noodles

INGREDIENTS

- [ ] 1 tbsp (15 mL) canola oil
- [ ] 4 cloves garlic, minced
- [ ] 1/2 yellow onion, sliced
- [ ] 1 tsp (5 mL) fresh ginger, minced
- [ ] 2 cups (500 mL) vegetable stock
- [ ] 2 tbsp (30 mL) white miso paste, divided
- [ ] 2 tbsp (30 mL) reduced-sodium soy sauce, divided
- [ ] 1 tbsp (15 mL) maple syrup
- [ ] 2 tsp (10 mL) lime juice
- [ ] 2 cups (8 oz/225 g) baby carrots, halved lengthwise
- [ ] 1 tbsp (15 mL) cornstarch
- [ ] 1 tsp (5 mL) pepper
- [ ] 14 oz (400 g) block firm tofu, pressed (see TIP below) and cubed
- [ ] 1 package (8 oz/225 g) ramen noodles
- [ ] 1 tbsp (15 mL) sesame oil
- [ ] A few sprigs fresh cilantro, for garnish

TIP: Pressing tofu makes the texture a bit chewier by lowering the water content. To do this easily, set the block of tofu on a paper towel lined plate, fold more paper towel to set on top and weigh it down with heavy books or cans for about 15 minutes.

Miso-glazed carrots, crisp tofu and chewy ramen noodles come together in a spicy stock. It's satisfying as a full meal, but add a vegetable boost of broccoli or cabbage to stretch it even further.

1. Preheat oven to 450°F (230°C).

2. In large saucepan over medium-high heat, warm canola oil. Sauté garlic, onion and ginger, 1 to 2 minutes to release the flavour.

3. Stir in vegetable stock, 1 tbsp (15 mL) of the miso paste and 1 tbsp (15 mL) of the soy sauce until blended.

4. Reduce heat and simmer stock mixture for 10 to 15 minutes.

5. In large bowl, whisk remaining miso paste and soy sauce, maple syrup and lime juice until blended and smooth. Toss in carrots to coat.

6. Evenly arrange the carrots in a single layer on one end of parchment paper–lined rimmed baking sheet.

7. In small bowl, whisk cornstarch with pepper, then toss in tofu to coat. Evenly arrange on remaining end of baking sheet.

8. Bake in oven until carrots are tender and tofu is crisp, 10 to 15 minutes.

9. Meanwhile, remove stock mixture from heat. Add noodles and let stand until rehydrated, about 3 to 4 minutes.

10. Divide stock and noodles between 2 serving dishes; add half each of the carrots and tofu. Drizzle with sesame oil; garnish with cilantro.

Makes 2 servings

VEGETARIAN · VEGAN · ASIAN (JAPANESE)

Black Bean & Garlic
Noodles

INGREDIENTS

- [ ] 1 tbsp (15 mL) vegetable oil
- [ ] 4 tsp (20 mL) ground ginger
- [ ] 1 head broccoli, chopped in florets and slices
- [ ] 1/2 cup (125 mL) water
- [ ] 1/2 cup (125 mL) button mushrooms, thinly sliced
- [ ] 4 oz (115 g) thick wheat noodles such as Korean Jajangmyeon noodles or linguini (1 1/2 inch diameter), cooked and drained
- [ ] 1/2 cup (125 mL) cashews, chopped

SAUCE

- [ ] 1/4 cup (60 mL) black bean garlic sauce
- [ ] 1 tbsp (15 mL) cornstarch mixed with 2 tbsp (30 mL) water
- [ ] 2 tsp (10 mL) Asian chili paste or hot sauce
- [ ] 2 tsp (10 mL) rice wine vinegar

Umami (umami is a flavour profile, not the name of the black bean sauce) flavours are the 'je ne sais quoi" of Asian cooking. The black bean sauce used in this recipe exemplifies it perfectly with its rich, earthy and meaty character. This paste of fermented beans, oil and sugar is found in the Asian or international section of most grocery stores. Go slowly when trying black bean sauce in other dishes — adding it bit by bit — as its flavour is scrumptious but pungent!

1. Sauce: In small bowl, stir together black bean garlic sauce, cornstarch, chili paste and vinegar until blended. Set aside.

2. In large frying pan over medium-high heat, warm oil. Stir-fry ginger until fragrant, 15 to 30 seconds.

3. Stir in broccoli and water. Cover and cook until tender-crisp, about 5 minutes.

4. Stir in mushrooms and sauce. Cook, stirring, until thickened.

5. Divide linguini between 2 serving dishes; top with broccoli mixture and garnish with cashews.

Makes 2 servings

> **VARIATION:**
> For a meaty alternative, add 6 oz (170 g) thinly sliced (against the grain) flank steak, to pan and stir-fry for 2 to 3 minutes before stirring in sauce.

VEGETARIAN

VEGAN

ASIAN (CHINESE)

vegetarian Miso
UDON NOODLES

INGREDIENTS

- [ ] 1 package (7 oz/200 g) udon noodles, cooked, rinsed and cooled
- [ ] 1 tbsp (15 mL) canola oil
- [ ] 1 clove garlic, minced or pressed
- [ ] ¼ yellow onion, thinly sliced
- [ ] 1-inch (2.5 cm) piece fresh ginger, minced
- [ ] ½ cup (125 mL) button mushrooms, thinly sliced
- [ ] 4 cups (1 L) vegetable stock
- [ ] 2 tbsp (30 mL) soy sauce
- [ ] 1 carrot, thinly sliced
- [ ] 1 cup (250 mL) packed baby spinach
- [ ] ¼ cup (60 mL) white miso paste
- [ ] 2 eggs
- [ ] Hot sauce (optional)

VARIATION:
To make a vegan version, substitute ½ cup (125 mL) cooked diced tofu for the egg.

We all know miso soup from the appetizing little bowlfuls served by restaurants before sushi. This key ingredient in Japanese cuisine is actually a fermented soybean paste that comes in a few different varieties; this recipe uses white miso, which is sweet and mild. You can find refrigerated miso in most grocery stores or at Asian markets.

1. Divide noodles between 2 serving bowls; set aside.

2. In large saucepan over medium-high heat, warm oil. Sauté garlic, onion and ginger just until softened, about 2 minutes.

3. Stir in mushrooms. Sauté for 3 to 4 minutes.

4. Stir in stock and soy sauce. Cook, scraping up brown bits from bottom of pan, for 2 to 3 minutes.

5. Stir in carrot, spinach and miso paste to combine. Reduce heat and simmer.

6. One at a time, carefully crack egg into small bowl or cup. Gently pour into simmering stock. Cook, without stirring, for 2 to 3 minutes (for soft yolk) or 4 minutes to cook through.

7. With slotted spoon, carefully transfer 1 egg to each serving dish over noodles. Gently ladle soup overtop. Serve with hot sauce (if using).

Makes 2 servings

VEGETARIAN

VEGAN

ASIAN (JAPANESE)

sweet & sour
PINEAPPLE CHICKEN

INGREDIENTS

SAUCE

- [ ] 4 cloves garlic, minced
- [ ] 1-inch (2.5 cm) piece fresh ginger, minced
- [ ] 1/3 cup (75 mL) chicken stock
- [ ] 1/4 cup (60 mL) packed brown sugar
- [ ] 1/4 cup (60 mL) rice vinegar
- [ ] 2 tbsp (30 mL) tomato paste
- [ ] 2 tbsp (30 mL) soy sauce
- [ ] 1 tbsp (15 mL) cornstarch

CHICKEN

- [ ] 1 egg
- [ ] 1/4 cup (60 mL) cornstarch
- [ ] 1/2 tsp (2 mL) black pepper
- [ ] 1 1/2 lb (675 g) boneless skinless chicken breast, cubed
- [ ] 1 tbsp (15 mL) sesame oil
- [ ] 2 sweet peppers, chopped
- [ ] 1 small yellow onion, chopped
- [ ] 1 cup (250 mL) fresh or drained canned pineapple
- [ ] 2 tbsp (30 mL) toasted sesame seeds, for garnish
- [ ] Sliced green onion, for garnish

This takeout favourite can easily be made at home and won't leave you ravenous an hour later. This dish is best served over fresh-cooked, steamy rice or noodles.

1. Sauce: In bowl, whisk garlic, ginger, chicken stock, brown sugar, vinegar, tomato paste, soy sauce and cornstarch; set aside.

2. In large bowl, whisk egg, cornstarch and pepper until blended; toss in chicken to coat.

3. In large non-stick frying pan over medium-high heat, warm oil; sauté chicken, until slightly crisp, golden brown and cooked through, about 5 to 6 minutes.

4. Gently stir in sauce to coat.

5. Gently toss in sweet peppers, onion and pineapple; sauté until sauce is thickened and gelled, about 3-4 minutes.

6. Transfer to serving dish; garnish with sesame seeds and green onion.

Makes 4 servings

VARIATION:
Try using extra-firm tofu in place of the chicken for a vegetarian alternative. Adding more vegetables will stretch this dish further; peas, carrots, corn and green beans are nutritious additions to this meal.

ASIAN (CHINESE)

yellow lentil, spinach &
CARROT DHAL

INGREDIENTS

- [ ] 2 tbsp (30 mL) vegetable oil, divided
- [ ] 2 cloves garlic, minced
- [ ] 1 cup (250 mL) chopped onions
- [ ] 1-inch (2.5 cm) piece fresh ginger, minced
- [ ] 1 tsp (5 mL) cinnamon
- [ ] 1 tsp (5 mL) ground coriander
- [ ] 1 tsp (5 mL) garam masala
- [ ] 1/2 tsp (2 mL) ground cumin
- [ ] 2 tomatoes, diced
- [ ] 1/2 jalapeño or mild chili pepper, seeded and diced
- [ ] 1 cup (250 mL) dried yellow lentils, rinsed
- [ ] 3 cups (750 mL) vegetable stock
- [ ] 2 carrots, cut in rounds
- [ ] 1/2 tbsp (7 mL) chili powder
- [ ] 2 cups (500 mL) packed baby spinach
- [ ] 2 tbsp (30 mL) lemon juice
- [ ] 1 cup (250 mL) plain yogurt
- [ ] 1/4 cup (60 mL) fresh cilantro, chopped

Spiced carrots kick up the flavour of the creamy lentils — this is Indian comfort food at its finest. Serve this hearty stew over rice or with a warm roti on the side. The flavour of this dish, as with many curries, improves as it rests — any leftovers will taste even better.

1. In large saucepan over medium-high heat, warm 1 tbsp (15 mL) of the oil. Sauté garlic and onions until golden.

2. Stir in ginger, cinnamon, coriander, garam masala and cumin to coat.

3. Stir in tomatoes, jalapeño and lentils. Sauté until heated through, 1 to 2 minutes.

4. Stir in vegetable stock. Reduce heat and simmer for 15 to 20 minutes.

5. In non-stick frying pan over medium-high heat, warm remaining oil; sauté carrots for 3 to 4 minutes. Toss in chili powder to coat.

6. Into simmering pan, stir spinach, and lemon juice just until spinach is wilted.

7. Divide evenly among 4 serving bowls. Divide carrots and yogurt overtop. Garnish with cilantro

Makes 4 servings

VEGETARIAN

VEGAN

INDIAN

VARIATION:
Substitute 1 1/2 cups cubed sweet potato or butternut squash for carrots.

MAKE AHEAD:
Cover and refrigerate for up to 3 to 4 days.

Red Lentil Dhal

INGREDIENTS

- ☐ 1 cup (250 mL) dried red lentils, rinsed and cleaned
- ☐ 2 tbsp (30 mL) vegetable oil, divided
- ☐ 2 cloves garlic, minced
- ☐ 1 cup (250 mL) chopped onions
- ☐ 1-inch (2.5 cm) piece fresh ginger, minced
- ☐ 1 tsp (5 mL) cinnamon
- ☐ 1 tsp (5 mL) ground coriander
- ☐ 1 tsp (5 mL) garam masala
- ☐ ¹/₂ tsp (2 mL) ground cumin
- ☐ ¹/₂ tsp (2 mL) curry powder
- ☐ 2 tomatoes, diced
- ☐ ¹/₂ jalapeño or mild chili pepper, seeded and diced
- ☐ 3 cups (750 mL) vegetable stock
- ☐ Salt and pepper to taste
- ☐ 1 cup (250 mL) plain yogurt
- ☐ ¹/₄ cup (60 mL) fresh cilantro, chopped
- ☐ 2 tbsp (30 mL) lemon juice

This super-simple dish is warming and filling and nourishing for body and soul. Serve it with rice alongside, or with naan to sop up the sauce. with some flavourful rice on the side, or with some naan to sop up the sauce.

1. In bowl, cover lentils with water; let soak for about 20 minutes. Rinse lentils well under running tap water until water runs clear. Drain and set aside.

2. In saucepan over medium-high heat, warm 1 tbsp (15 mL) of the oil. Sauté garlic and onions until golden.

3. Stir in ginger, cinnamon, coriander, garam masala, cumin and curry, to coat.

4. Stir in tomatoes, jalapeños and lentils; cook, stirring, until heated through, about 1 minute.

5. Stir in vegetable stock. Reduce heat and simmer for 20 minutes.

6. Whisk to break up lentils and thicken soup; add salt and pepper.

7. Evenly divide among 4 serving dishes; spoon one-quarter of the yogurt over each. Sprinkle cilantro overtop; drizzle with lemon juice.

Makes 4 servings

MAKE AHEAD:
Cover and refrigerate for up to 4 days or freeze for up to 4 to 6 months.

VEGETARIAN

VEGAN

INDIAN

Bigger, Better
VEGETABLE & QUINOA BIRYANI

INGREDIENTS

- [ ] 2 tbsp (30 mL) vegetable oil
- [ ] 3 cloves garlic, minced
- [ ] 2 cups (500 mL) chopped onions
- [ ] 1 large sweet potato, cubed
- [ ] 1 small head cauliflower, broken in small florets
- [ ] 1 jalapeño or mild chili pepper, seeded and diced
- [ ] 3 tbsp (45 mL) curry paste
- [ ] 1 tsp (5 mL) dry mustard seeds
- [ ] 3 cups (750 mL) vegetable stock, heated
- [ ] 1 1/2 cups (375 mL) uncooked quinoa, washed
- [ ] 1 cup (250 mL) frozen peas
- [ ] 1 cup (250 mL) frozen corn
- [ ] 1/2 cup (125 mL) salted roasted cashews
- [ ] 1/2 cup (125 mL) packed fresh cilantro leaves, chopped
- [ ] 2 tbsp (30 mL) lemon juice
- [ ] Salt and pepper to taste
- [ ] 1 cup (250 mL) plain yogurt

VARIATION:
To sweeten things up, add 1/4 cup (60 mL) raisins along with quinoa.

Classic biryani is a complicated dish to cook — worth it, but complicated. This one-pot version has all the flavour of the traditional take, but makes it healthier, more filling and easier. Serving with a generous dollop of plain tangy yogurt is strongly recommended.

1. Preheat oven to 400°F (200°C).

2. In large, lidded, oven-proof saucepan over medium-high heat, warm oil. Sauté garlic and onions until golden. Remove spoonful of garlic mixture and set aside.

3. Into pan, stir sweet potato and cauliflower. Sauté just until tender, about 5 minutes.

4. Push mixture to edge of pan. In centre of pan, stir together jalapeño, curry paste and mustard. Toast for about 3 minutes or until the mustard seeds are sputtering.

5. Stir in vegetable stock, quinoa, peas and corn until combined. Bring to a simmer.

6. Cover and transfer to oven. Bake until quinoa is tender and grains are edged with white, about 20 minutes.

7. Stir in cashews, cilantro, lemon juice, salt, pepper and reserved garlic mixture.

8. Divide evenly among 4 serving dishes; top with yogurt.

Makes 4 servings

VEGETARIAN

VEGAN

INDIAN

Quinoa, sweet potato
& Pea Samosa Bowl

INGREDIENTS

- ☐ 1 large sweet potato, diced
- ☐ 2 tbsp (30 mL) coconut oil or ghee, melted
- ☐ 2 tsp (10 mL) curry powder
- ☐ ¹/₂ tsp (2 mL) ground cumin
- ☐ ¹/₂ tbsp (7 mL) brown mustard seeds
- ☐ 1 small yellow onion, diced
- ☐ 1-inch (2.5 cm) piece fresh ginger, grated (or 1 tbsp/15 mL ground ginger)
- ☐ 2 cups (500 mL) low-sodium vegetable or beef stock
- ☐ 1 cup (250 mL) uncooked quinoa
- ☐ 1 cup (250 mL) frozen baby peas
- ☐ ¹/₂ cup (125 mL) store-bought mango chutney
- ☐ ¹/₂ cup (125 mL) fresh cilantro, chopped

Spicy sweet potatoes, earthy quinoa and plump peas bring all of the comforting goodness of a samosa to this healthful and hearty vegan meal. Think of this dish as a detox for your organs — full of cleansing spices, fibre, protein, healthy fats and — oh yes — flavour!

1. Preheat oven to 400°F (200°C).

2. In bowl, toss together sweet potato, coconut oil, curry powder and cumin to coat; evenly spread over rimmed baking sheet. Bake in oven, stirring occasionally, until golden brown, 5 to 10 minutes.

3. In dry large saucepan over medium-high heat, toast mustard seeds, shaking pan occasionally, until most are popped, about 2 minutes.

4. Stir in onion, ginger, beef stock and quinoa. Reduce heat and simmer covered until quinoa is tender and grains are edged with white.

5. Stir in peas and cook until heated through.

6. Divide among 4 serving bowls; top with one-quarter each of the sweet potato mixture and chutney. Garnish with cilantro.

Makes 4 servings

VEGETARIAN

VEGAN

INDIAN

Chana Masala

VEGETARIAN

INDIAN

INGREDIENTS

- [ ] 2 tbsp (30 mL) canola oil
- [ ] 1 large onion, diced
- [ ] 4 cloves garlic, minced
- [ ] 1-inch (2.5 cm) piece fresh ginger, minced
- [ ] 1 green chili pepper, seeded and finely diced
- [ ] 2 tsp (10 mL) chili powder
- [ ] 2 tsp (10 mL) garam masala
- [ ] 1 tsp (15 mL) cumin seeds
- [ ] 1 tsp (5 mL) ground coriander
- [ ] 1 tsp (5 mL) turmeric
- [ ] 1 can (14 oz/ 398 mL) chickpeas, drained and rinsed
- [ ] 1 can (28 oz/796 mL) crushed tomatoes, with juice
- [ ] 1 cup (250 mL) water or vegetable broth
- [ ] 1 tbsp (15 mL) packed brown sugar
- [ ] 1 tbsp (15 mL) lemon juice
- [ ] Plain yogurt, for garnish (optional)
- [ ] Fresh cilantro leaves, for garnish (optional)

A popular street food and favourite Indian curry, this super-healthy dish is great to batch-cook and eat later as a main dish or a satisfying snack during a busy week. Chickpeas are a great (and inexpensive!) source of protein and fibre, while the spices and aromatics offer in-your-face bold flavour. Try it with grated Parmesan and pasta, over rice, or topped with poached eggs for a protein-packed breakfast.

1. In large saucepan over medium-high heat, warm oil. Sauté onion just until softened, 3 to 4 minutes.

2. Stir in garlic and ginger. Sauté for 1 to 2 minutes.

3. Stir in chili pepper, chili powder, garam masala, cumin seeds, coriander and turmeric. Sauté until toasted and fragrant, 1 to 2 minutes.

4. Stir in chickpeas, tomatoes, water and brown sugar. Reduce heat and simmer for 10 to 15 minutes.

5. Stir in lemon juice.

6. Divide among 4 serving bowls. Top each with spoonful of yogurt and garnish with cilantro (if using).

Makes: 4 servings

TIPS

A common technique in Indian recipes, frying or toasting spices boosts their flavour.
Purchase rarely-used spices in small quantities, and store in airtight containers in a cool dry space, so they stay fresh and flavourful.

MAKE AHEAD:

Transfer cooked garlic mixture to slow cooker; stir in remaining ingredients (except yogurt and cilantro) and cook on low for 4 to 6 hours. Add toppings before serving.

Cashew Chicken Korma

INGREDIENTS

- [ ] $^1/_2$ cup (125 mL) cashews
- [ ] 2 tbsp (30 mL) canola oil, divided
- [ ] 2 small onions, sliced
- [ ] 2 chili peppers, seeded and diced
- [ ] 2 cloves garlic, minced
- [ ] 1-inch (2.5 cm) piece fresh ginger, grated (or 1 tbsp/15 mL ground ginger)
- [ ] 2 tsp (10 mL) garam masala
- [ ] 2 tsp (10 mL) ground coriander
- [ ] Pinch nutmeg
- [ ] 7 oz (200 g) boneless skinless chicken breasts, cubed
- [ ] 1$^1/_2$ cups (375 mL) low-sodium chicken stock
- [ ] $^1/_4$ cup (60 mL) yellow raisins (optional)
- [ ] $^1/_2$ cup (125 mL) plain Greek yogurt
- [ ] 1 tbsp (15 mL) lime juice
- [ ] Plain yogurt, for garnish (optional)
- [ ] Fresh cilantro leaves, for garnish (optional)

Silky cashew-and-onion purée make this dish delightfully smooth without the traditional butterfat. If cashews aren't your favourite, use almonds or sunflower seeds instead.

1. In dry large saucepan over medium heat, toast cashews, shaking pan constantly to prevent burning, for about 4 minutes.

2. Transfer to food processor and set aside.

3. In pan, warm 1 tbsp (15 mL) of the oil. Sauté onions until golden brown, about 10 minutes.

4. Transfer to food processor with cashews; purée until blended and smooth.

5. In pan, warm remaining oil. Toss in chili peppers, garlic, ginger, garam masala, coriander and nutmeg. Sauté for 1 to 2 minutes.

6. Stir in chicken to coat. Sauté until browned.

7. Stir in chicken stock and raisins (if using), scraping up brown bits from bottom of pan.

8. Stir in onion purée. Reduce heat and simmer until thickened, about 5 minutes.

9. Stir in Greek yogurt and lime juice just until heated through. Garnish with yogurt and cilantro (if using).

Makes 4 servings

INDIAN

Red Pepper
Yellow Curry

INGREDIENTS

- [ ] 2 tbsp (30 mL) canola oil
- [ ] 2 cloves garlic, minced
- [ ] 1 large onion, chopped
- [ ] 1-inch (2.5 cm) piece fresh ginger grated (or 1 tbsp/15 mL ground ginger)
- [ ] 3 small white potatoes, diced
- [ ] 2 carrots, chopped in rounds
- [ ] 1 red sweet pepper, sliced in strips
- [ ] 2 tsp (10 mL) chili powder
- [ ] 1 tbsp (15 mL) curry powder
- [ ] 1/2 tsp (2 mL) turmeric
- [ ] Pinch red pepper flakes
- [ ] 1 can (14 oz/398 mL) coconut milk
- [ ] 1 tbsp (15 mL) liquid honey
- [ ] Fresh cilantro leaves, for garnish

This easy, savoury stew filled with Indian spices has a heavenly aroma, and makes a perfect pairing with grilled fish or tofu and a hearty slice of multigrain bread.

1. In large saucepan over medium-high heat, warm oil. Sauté garlic, onions and ginger for 2 to 3 minutes.

2. Toss in potatoes and carrots. Sauté until tender and golden, about 5 minutes.

3. Stir in red pepper, chili powder, curry powder, turmeric and red pepper flakes.

4. Whisk in coconut milk, scraping up brown bits from bottom of pan. Reduce heat and simmer for about 10 minutes.

5. Stir in honey. Garnish with cilantro (if using).

Makes 4 servings

VEGETARIAN

VEGAN

INDIAN

Curried
Potato, Cauliflower & Peas

INGREDIENTS

- [ ] 2 tbsp (30 mL) brown mustard seeds
- [ ] 2 cloves garlic, minced
- [ ] 1 large onion, chopped
- [ ] 1-inch (2.5 cm) piece fresh ginger, grated (or 1 tbsp/15 mL ground ginger)
- [ ] 2 tbsp (30 mL) canola oil or ghee
- [ ] 1 tsp (5 mL) ground cumin
- [ ] 1 tsp (5 mL) garam masala
- [ ] $1/2$ tsp (2 mL) turmeric
- [ ] $1/2$ tsp (2 mL) cayenne pepper
- [ ] 3 small white potatoes, diced
- [ ] 2 cups (500 mL) cauliflower florets
- [ ] 1 cup (250 mL) water
- [ ] 1 cup (250 mL) frozen baby peas
- [ ] $1/2$ cup (125) fresh cilantro leaves, chopped

Mustard seeds bring a deep, earthy element to this spicy dish. Serve it fresh-cooked on its own, or cooled as a substitute for summertime potato salad.

1. In dry large saucepan over medium-high heat, toast mustard seeds, shaking pan, until most have popped, about 2 minutes.

2. Stir in garlic, onion, garlic, ginger, oil, cumin, garam masala, turmeric and cayenne pepper. Sauté until fragrant, about 2 minutes. Stir in potatoes and cauliflower to coat.

3. Stir in water. Cover, reduce heat and simmer until potatoes are tender, about 10 minutes.

4. Stir in peas and cilantro leaves, cook until just heated through, about 1 minute.

Makes 4 servings

VEGETARIAN

VEGAN

INDIAN

Zucchini, Tomato
& Chickpea Curry with Couscous

INGREDIENTS

- [ ] 2 tbsp (30 mL) vegetable or coconut oil
- [ ] 2 cloves garlic, minced
- [ ] 1 small white onion, diced
- [ ] 1 tbsp (15 mL) ground cumin
- [ ] 1 tsp (5 mL) ground coriander
- [ ] 1 tsp (5 mL) curry powder
- [ ] 1/4 tsp (1 mL) ground allspice
- [ ] 1/4 tsp (1 mL) cinnamon
- [ ] Pinch red pepper flakes
- [ ] 4 tomatoes, diced
- [ ] 2 small zucchini, diced
- [ ] 1 can (14 oz/398 mL) chickpeas, drained and rinsed
- [ ] 1 cup (250 mL) water or stock
- [ ] 1 tbsp (15 mL) lemon juice
- [ ] 1/4 cup (60 mL) fresh tarragon, chopped
- [ ] 4 cups (1 L) cooked couscous
- [ ] Tarragon leaves, for garnish (optional)

This vegan stew brims with healthful vegetables, aromatics and spices in a savoury stock. Lemon juice, added at the end of cooking, enhances the flavour without additional salt. Try poaching an egg or two or even some fresh fish in the stock for an added protein boost to the meal.

1. In large saucepan over medium-high heat, warm oil; sauté garlic and onion for 3 to 4 minutes.

2. Stir in cumin, coriander, curry powder, allspice, cinnamon and red pepper flakes.

3. Stir in tomatoes and zucchini. Cover, reduce heat and simmer until tomatoes thicken into sauce, 3 to 4 minutes.

4. Stir in chickpeas and water. Simmer for 5 minutes.

5. Stir in lemon juice and chopped tarragon.

6. Serve over couscous; garnish with additional tarragon leaves (if using).

Makes 4 servings

VEGETARIAN

VEGAN

INDIAN

Curried Eggplant
WITH TOMATO & BASIL

INGREDIENTS

- [ ] 2 tbsp (30 mL) vegetable oil
- [ ] 2 cloves garlic, minced
- [ ] 1 eggplant (about 1 lb/450 g)
- [ ] 1 large onion, diced
- [ ] 1 tbsp (15 mL) curry powder
- [ ] 2 lb (900 g) tomatoes, diced
- [ ] 1 can (14 oz/398 mL) chickpeas, drained and rinsed
- [ ] 2 cups (500 mL) water or low-sodium vegetable stock
- [ ] $1/2$ cup (125 mL) fresh basil leaves, torn
- [ ] Fresh basil leaves, for garnish (optional)

How did eggplant become the ugly stepchild of the produce section? The dark purple exterior is rich with antioxidants and the flesh is creamy and velvety. Try serving this curry over a piping hot bowl of basmati rice or with a piece of naan and a generous dollop of yogurt.

1. In large saucepan over medium-high heat, warm oil. Sauté garlic, eggplant, onion and curry powder until onion is softened, 3 to 4 minutes.

2. Stir in tomatoes, chickpeas and water. Cover, reduce heat and simmer until eggplant is tender, about 10 minutes.

3. Stir in torn basil. Garnish with basil leaves (if using).

Makes 4 servings

VEGETARIAN

VEGAN

INDIAN

MAKE AHEAD:
Sauté garlic, eggplant, onion and curry powder just until golden, 2 to 3 minutes. Transfer to slow cooker, stir in remaining ingredients; cook on low for 4 to 6 hours.

Chicken, potato &
Spinach Balti

INGREDIENTS

- [ ] 2 cloves garlic, minced
- [ ] 1/2 small chili pepper, seeded and diced
- [ ] 1-inch (2.5 cm) piece fresh ginger, minced
- [ ] 1/4 cup (60 mL) plain yogurt + extra for garnish
- [ ] 2 tbsp (30 mL) lime juice
- [ ] 1/2 tsp (2 mL) ground coriander
- [ ] 1/2 tsp (2 mL) ground turmeric
- [ ] 1/2 tsp (2 mL) ground cumin
- [ ] 2 boneless, skinless chicken breasts or thighs, cubed
- [ ] 1 tbsp (15 mL) canola oil or ghee
- [ ] 2 unpeeled white potatoes, diced
- [ ] 1 large onion, diced
- [ ] 2 tomatoes, diced
- [ ] 2 tbsp (30 mL) tomato paste
- [ ] 1/2 cup (125 mL) water
- [ ] 3 cups (750 mL) baby spinach
- [ ] 1/2 cup (125 mL) half-and-half cream (10%)
- [ ] 4 cups (1 L) cooked rice
- [ ] 1/4 cup (60 mL) fresh cilantro, chopped

Balti is named after the traditional metal pot that is used from start to finish in this recipe. Balti is not a curry that is slowly cooked and simmered for hours, it's best if it's cooked quickly and the vegetables still have a bit of crunch. Adjust the sauce with water to match your preferred thickness, and try swapping out the vegetables with what you have on hand.

1. In large bowl, stir together garlic, chili pepper, ginger, yogurt, lime juice, coriander, turmeric and cumin. Toss in chicken to coat.

2. Set aside. Let marinate for 10 to 15 minutes (or transfer to resealable plastic bag and refrigerate for up to 2 hours).

3. In large saucepan over medium-high heat, warm oil. Sauté potatoes and onion until softened, 5 to 6 minutes.

4. Stir in tomatoes, tomato paste and water to blend and coat.

5. Stir in chicken and marinade, reduce heat and simmer until chicken is cooked through and no longer pink in centre, about 10 minutes.

6. Reduce heat to low. Stir in spinach and cream and cook, stirring, until spinach has wilted and entire dish is heated through.

7. Transfer to serving bowl over rice; garnish with yogurt and cilantro.

Makes 4 servings

MAKE AHEAD:
Marinate chicken in a reuseable plastic bag ahead of time for quick assembly later on.

Coconut Chana Saag
CHICKPEAS & RICE

INGREDIENTS

- [ ] 2 tbsp (30 mL) vegetable or coconut oil
- [ ] 2 cloves garlic, minced
- [ ] 1 large onion, diced
- [ ] 2-inch (5 cm) piece fresh ginger, minced
- [ ] 1 tbsp (15 mL) curry powder
- [ ] 1 tsp (5 mL) ground cumin
- [ ] 3 or 4 tomatoes, diced
- [ ] 1 can (14 oz/398 mL) chickpeas, drained and rinsed
- [ ] 2 cups (500 mL) fresh or thawed frozen lacinato kale leaves, chopped
- [ ] 1/2 cup (125 mL) water
- [ ] 1 can (14 oz/398 mL) coconut milk
- [ ] 2 tbsp (30 mL) lime juice
- [ ] Salt and pepper to taste
- [ ] Fresh cilantro sprigs, for garnish
- [ ] 4 cups (1 L) cooked basmati rice

Although this recipe is called 'chana saag" (literally 'chickpeas spinach"), here the spinach is swapped for its more hearty relative, kale. The kale leaf is a bit more rigid, so it doesn't get mushy from the acidic tomatoes, spices and heat of the dish. If kale is not your thing, collard greens or Swiss chard work just as well.

1. In large saucepan over medium-high heat, warm oil. Sauté garlic, onion and ginger until onion is softened, 3 to 4 minutes.

2. Stir in curry powder and cumin. Sauté for 2 to 3 minutes.

3. Stir in tomatoes. Reduce heat and simmer until tomatoes break down and become soft, about 5 minutes.

4. Stir in chickpeas, kale and water. Simmer until most of the water has been absorbed.

5. Stir in coconut milk, lime juice, salt and pepper. Garnish with cilantro; serve with rice on side.

Makes 4 servings

VEGETARIAN

VEGAN

INDIAN

Crunchy Curried
Cabbage, Carrot & Peas

INGREDIENTS

- [ ] 2 tbsp (30 mL) brown mustard seeds
- [ ] 2 cloves garlic, minced
- [ ] 1 large onion, chopped
- [ ] 1-inch (2.5 cm) piece fresh ginger, grated (or 1 tbsp/15 mL ground ginger)
- [ ] 2 tbsp (30 mL) canola oil or ghee
- [ ] 1 tsp (5 mL) ground cumin
- [ ] 1 tsp (5 mL) garam masala
- [ ] ½ tsp (2 mL) turmeric
- [ ] ½ tsp (2 mL) cayenne pepper
- [ ] 3 small white potatoes, diced
- [ ] 2 cups (500 mL) cauliflower florets
- [ ] 1 cup (250 mL) water
- [ ] 1 cup (250 mL) frozen baby peas
- [ ] Salt and pepper to taste
- [ ] Fresh cilantro leaves, for garnish

A flavourful side dish that's inexpensive to make and super-nutritious. The simple cabbage is a versatile vegetable that compliments bold curry spices.

1. In dry large saucepan over medium-high heat, toast mustard seeds, shaking pan, until most are popped, about 2 minutes.

2. Stir in garlic, onion, ginger, oil, cumin, garam masala, turmeric and cayenne pepper. Sauté until fragrant, about 2 minutes.

3. Stir in potatoes and cauliflower to coat. Stir in water, reduce heat, cover and simmer until potatoes are tender, about 10 minutes.

4. Stir in peas until heated through. Stir in salt and pepper. Garnish with cilantro leaves.

Makes 4 servings

VEGETARIAN

VEGAN

INDIAN

African peanut stew

INGREDIENTS

- [ ] 2 tbsp (30 mL) canola oil
- [ ] 2 large cloves garlic, minced
- [ ] 1 small red onion, diced
- [ ] 1 ¹/₂ inch (4 cm) piece fresh ginger, minced
- [ ] 1 large sweet potato, cubed
- [ ] Pinch red pepper flakes
- [ ] 5 cups (1.25 L) vegetable stock
- [ ] 1 can (14 oz / 398 mL) chickpeas, drained and rinsed
- [ ] 1 can (28 oz / 796 mL) crushed tomatoes, with juice
- [ ] 1 cup (250 mL) fresh or thawed frozen kale leaves, chopped
- [ ] 1 cup (250 mL) chunky natural peanut butter
- [ ] 2 tbsp (30 mL) packed brown sugar
- [ ] Salt and pepper to taste

When you need a comforting hug for your soul, this is the recipe to turn to. This hearty meal — that's easy and good for you — is composed of heart-healthy fats and antioxidant-rich superfoods. Try serving this over couscous or brown rice, and don't forget to freeze leftovers (if there is any!).

1. In large saucepan over medium-high heat, warm oil. Sauté garlic, onion and ginger until onion is softened, 3 to 4 minutes.

2. Toss in sweet potato and red pepper flakes to coat.

3. Sauté until sweet potato is heated through.

4. Stir in vegetable stock and chickpeas. Reduce heat and simmer until sweet potato is tender, about 15 minutes.

5. Stir in tomatoes, kale, peanut butter, brown sugar, salt and pepper until peanut butter is blended. Simmer, stirring, until heated through, 10 to 15 minutes.

Makes 4 servings

VEGETARIAN

VEGAN

AFRICAN

VARIATION:
For a meaty alternative, omit chickpeas and add 1 lb (450 g) lean beef, sliced thinly at the same stage as the sweet potatoes are added, and use beef stock instead of vegetable stock.

MAKE AHEAD:
Cover and refrigerate for up to 3 days or freeze for longer storage.

Slow Cooker Chicken
TIKKA MASALA

INGREDIENTS

- [ ] Cooking spray, for slow cooker
- [ ] 1 lb (450 g) boneless skinless chicken thighs, cubed
- [ ] 1/2 cup (125 mL) half-and-half (10%) cream
- [ ] Plain yogurt, for garnish (optional)
- [ ] Fresh cilantro leaves, chopped, for garnish (optional)
- [ ] 4 cups (1 L) cooked brown rice

SAUCE

- [ ] 2 tbsp (30 mL) canola oil
- [ ] 4 cloves garlic, minced
- [ ] 1 large onion, diced
- [ ] 1-inch (2.5 cm) piece fresh ginger, minced
- [ ] 1 tbsp (15 mL) garam masala
- [ ] 2 tsp (10 mL) paprika
- [ ] 1 tsp (5 mL) curry powder
- [ ] 1/2 tsp (2 mL) cinnamon
- [ ] Pinch of red pepper flakes
- [ ] 1 can (28 oz/796 mL) crushed tomatoes, with juice
- [ ] 2 tbsp (30 mL) tomato paste
- [ ] 1 tbsp (15 mL) packed brown sugar
- [ ] 1 tbsp (15 mL) lemon juice
- [ ] 1 cup (250 mL) plain yogurt

One dish that's a given for any Indian restaurant is chicken tikka masala. Chunks of chicken wrapped in a smooth, spiced tomato sauce strikes all the comfort nerves. The best part? Coming home after a long day to find a supper that's pure perfection awaiting your arrival.

1. Sauce: In large saucepan over medium-high heat, warm oil; sauté garlic, onion and ginger until onion is softened and golden.

2. Stir in garam masala, paprika, curry powder, cinnamon and red pepper flakes. Sauté until toasted and fragrant, about 2 minutes.

3. Stir in tomatoes, tomato paste, brown sugar and lemon juice to combine. Remove from heat.

4. Whisk in yogurt until blended and smooth.

5. Coat slow cooker with cooking spray. Evenly arrange chicken over bottom; pour sauce overtop.

6. Cook on high for 4 to 6 hours. Then uncover and cook until thickened, about 15 minutes. Stir in cream.

7. Transfer to serving dish. Garnish with yogurt (if using) and cilantro. Serve with rice on side.

Makes 6 to 8 servings

VEGETARIAN

INDIAN

Slow Cooker Chicken
CURRY WITH GINGERED YOGURT

INGREDIENTS

- [ ] 2 tbsp (30 mL) canola oil, divided
- [ ] 2 cloves garlic, minced
- [ ] 1 large onion, chopped
- [ ] 2 tbsp (30 mL) curry powder
- [ ] 1/2 tsp (2 mL) turmeric
- [ ] Pinch red pepper flakes
- [ ] 1 can (14 oz / 398 mL) coconut milk
- [ ] 1 can (14 oz / 398 mL) low-sodium tomato sauce
- [ ] 2 boneless skinless chicken breasts, cubed
- [ ] 2 cups (500 mL) sweet potato, cubed
- [ ] 2 cups (500 mL) cooked basmati rice
- [ ] 1/4 cup (60 mL) fresh cilantro, chopped

TOPPING

- [ ] 1 cup (250 mL) plain yogurt
- [ ] 1 tbsp (15 mL) fresh ginger, grated
- [ ] 2 tbsp (30 mL) liquid honey
- [ ] 1 tbsp (15 mL) lemon juice

Slow cooker curries are especially warming during the winter months, but also great hot meals to cook without overheating a small apartment in the summer. Once you try this gingered-yogurt topping, you'll be making extra to serve with fresh fruit as dessert.

1. Topping: In bowl, whisk yogurt, ginger, honey and lemon juice until blended and smooth. Cover and refrigerate until ready to use.

2. In large saucepan over medium-high heat, warm oil. Sauté garlic, onion, curry powder, turmeric and red pepper flakes for 2 to 3 minutes.

3. Scrape into slow cooker.

4. Stir in coconut milk and tomato sauce to combine. Toss in chicken and sweet potato.

5. Cook on low for 6 to 8 hours.

6. Divide rice evenly among 4 serving bowls; top each with 1/4 of the curry, then 1/4 of the topping. Garnish with cilantro.

Makes 4 servings

VEGETARIAN

INDIAN

Chicken & sweet
Potato Coconut Curry

VEGAN

INDIAN

INGREDIENTS

- [ ] 2 tablespoons (30 mL) coconut oil
- [ ] 3 tbsp (45 mL) curry powder
- [ ] 1 small onion, diced
- [ ] 2 large cloves garlic, minced
- [ ] 1 1/2 inch (1 cm) fresh ginger, minced
- [ ] 1 large or 2 medium sweet potato, cut into cubes
- [ ] 1 tbsp (15 mL) crushed red pepper
- [ ] 1 lb (16 oz/454 g) chicken thighs, cubed
- [ ] 1 1/2 cups (398 mL) can coconut milk
- [ ] 1 cup (250 mL) chicken stock
- [ ] 1/2 tsp (3 mL) salt
- [ ] 2 tbsp (30 mL) packed brown sugar
- [ ] 1/4 cup (60 mL) cilantro leaves, chopped
- [ ] 1/4 cup (60 mL) sweetened desiccated coconut

The sweetness of the sweet potato combined with the creamy coconut is a perfect balance for curry spices. Try serving this dish with a few cilantro sprigs and some toasted coconut.

1. Pour oil into a medium saucepan over medium-high heat. Using a wooden spoon, stir in onion, garlic, and ginger, and sauté until it begins to soften or about 3 to 4 minutes. Toss in sweet potato, chicken, crushed red pepper and curry spice, stirring again to coat the ingredients in oil and release a bit of steam.

2. Once sweet potatoes have been heated through and the chicken is crisp on the edges, pour the coconut milk over the mixture and use a spoon to deglaze the bottom of the pot. Stir in the stock and bring the pot to a gentle simmer for 15 minutes or until the sweet potato is fork tender. Stir in the brown sugar and return to a simmer.

3. Toast the coconut by placing it in a non-stick pan over medium-high heat. Shake the pan lightly to move the coconut around the pan to prevent burning. Remove the coconut from the pan as soon as it is golden and fragrant and sprinkle over the curry.

4. Serve a bowl of this stew piping hot, garnished with cilantro and toasted coconut.

Makes 4 servings

VARIATION:
For a vegan alternative substitute chickpeas instead of chicken and use vegetable broth instead of chicken.

MAKE AHEAD:
Cover and refrigerate up to 3 days, or freeze for longer storage.

Butternut squash
Mac 'n' Cheese

INGREDIENTS

- [ ] 4 tbsp (60 mL) butter, divided
- [ ] 2 large cloves garlic, minced
- [ ] 1 small onion, diced
- [ ] 1 can (14 oz/398 mL) butternut squash purée (or 2 cups/500 mL fresh or thawed frozen diced squash, microwaved until tender and mashed)
- [ ] 2 cups (500 mL) 1% milk, divided
- [ ] 1 tbsp (15 mL) packed brown sugar
- [ ] 1/2 tsp (2 mL) red pepper flakes
- [ ] 1/2 tsp (2 mL) salt
- [ ] 2 tbsp (30 mL) all-purpose flour
- [ ] 1 1/2 cups (375 mL) 1% milk
- [ ] 2 cups (500 mL) macaroni pasta, cooked and drained
- [ ] 2 cups (500 mL) shredded cheddar cheese

> **TIPS:**
> Cooking onion slowly caramelizes it, which brings a sweet, smoky flavour to the dish. It's worth the wait.
> **VARIATION:**
> Preheat oven to 400°F (200°C). After folding in cheese, scrape macaroni mixture into greased baking dish. In small bowl with fork, stir together 1/2 cup (125 mL) panko or Italian-seasoned bread crumbs and 2 tbsp (30 mL)

Butternut squash adds smoothness and subtle sweetness to this healthy, whole-food spin on classic comfort food. Think of this as an adult version of your childhood favourite. Get creative by swapping cheeses, using different pasta or sprinkling in some savoury herbs such as dried thyme or sage to punch up the flavour.

1. In non-stick saucepan over medium-high heat, melt 3 tbsp (45 mL) butter.

2. Using a plastic whisk, whisk in the flour and stir to form a paste.

3. Whisk in the milk until combined and simmer over low heat, stirring every so often, while the sauce thickens.

4. In large saucepan over low heat, heat the remaining butter and sauté garlic and onion until golden brown, about 5 minutes.

5. Stir in the squash and the warmed milk and butter mixture until blended and smooth.

6. Stir in brown sugar, red pepper flakes and salt until blended.

7. Fold in the macaroni. Fold in cheese.

8. Cook, stirring, until cheese is melted, sauce is thickened and macaroni is heated through, about 5 minutes.

Makes 4 servings

melted butter to coat; sprinkle these crumbs evenly over macaroni mixture. Bake in oven until topping is golden and cheese is bubbling, about 15 minutes.
MAKE AHEAD:
Cover and refrigerate for up to 4 days or freeze for up to 1 month.

VEGETARIAN

ITALIAN

Asparagus & Fried Egg
SPAGHETTI

INGREDIENTS

- [ ] 7 oz (200 g) spaghetti pasta
- [ ] 2 tbsp (30 mL) olive oil
- [ ] 1/2 small yellow onion, diced
- [ ] 2 cloves garlic, sliced
- [ ] Pinch red pepper flakes
- [ ] 1 cup (250 mL) chopped trimmed asparagus
- [ ] 2 eggs
- [ ] 2 cups (500 mL) baby spinach
- [ ] 1/2 cup (125 mL) grated Parmesan cheese
- [ ] Parmesan cheese garnish (optional)

Fried eggs, asparagus and pasta may sound like an odd combination, but — trust me — it works. If you want to up the ante with a fancy presentation, skip tossing the eggs with the pasta, and serve the dish with an over easy egg proudly displayed on top of each serving. Gooey yellow yolk seductively oozing over the plate is optional but definitely recommended.

1. In large pot of boiling salted water, cook spaghetti. Drain, reserving 1/2 cup (125 mL) cooking water in a separate container.

2. Return spaghetti to pot and keep warm.

3. In frying pan over medium-high heat, warm oil. Sauté onion just until golden, about 4 minutes.

4. Stir in garlic and red pepper flakes. Sauté for about 2 minutes.

5. Stir in asparagus, then crack eggs into pan. Cook, stirring, until egg whites are set and asparagus is bright green.

6. Over medium-low heat, toss into spaghetti. Toss in spinach and Parmesan to coat, adding reserved cooking water, if necessary, to achieve desired consistency.

7. Transfer to serving dish; top with more cheese.

Makes 2 servings

VEGETARIAN

ITALIAN

Tomato, Basil &
SHRIMP LINGUINE

INGREDIENTS

- [ ] 8 oz (225 g) linguini pasta
- [ ] 4 tbsp (60 mL) olive oil, divided
- [ ] 1 lb (450 g) shrimp, deveined, tails removed
- [ ] 2 cloves garlic, minced
- [ ] 2 cups (500 mL) grape tomatoes
- [ ] 2 tbsp (30 mL) liquid honey
- [ ] Pinch red pepper flakes
- [ ] 1 ¹/₂ cups (375 mL) torn fresh basil leaves + more for garnish
- [ ] ¹/₂ lemon, cut in 4 wedges (optional)

Summery tomato and basil team up for the win in this fast pasta dish that's nothing short of sophisticated. Try making this dish your own by adding some fresh seasonal notes to the mix — garlic scapes, tender green peas and zucchini flowers are great options.

1. In large pot of boiling salted water, cook linguini; drain, separately reserving ¹/₂ cup (125 mL) cooking water.

2. Return lingiuini to pot and keep warm.

3. In frying pan over medium-high heat, warm 2 tbsp (30 mL) of the oil. Sauté shrimp until no longer opaque about 3 minutes.

4. With slotted spoon, transfer to small bowl. Set aside.

5. In pan, warm remaining oil; stir in garlic, tomatoes, honey, red pepper flakes and reserved cooking water. Reduce heat and simmer until tomatoes split and thicken into sauce, about 5 minutes.

6. Toss in linguini and shrimp. Cook, stirring, until heated through.

7. Transfer to serving plate. Garnish with basil. Serve with lemon wedges on side.

Makes 4 servings

ITALIAN

Cauliflower, Bacon
& Spaghetti Carbonara

INGREDIENTS

- [ ] 8 oz (225 g) spaghetti pasta
- [ ] 1 head cauliflower, chopped
- [ ] 4 cloves garlic, pressed
- [ ] 1/2 tsp (2 mL) black pepper
- [ ] 3 eggs, beaten
- [ ] 1/2 cup (125 mL) grated Parmesan cheese + more for garnish
- [ ] 6 slices bacon, diced and cooked, reserving fat in pan
- [ ] 1/4 cup (60 mL) parsley, chopped

Smoky bacon fat caramelizes the cauliflower, enhancing its nutty flavour in this yummy pasta.

1. In large pot of boiling salted water, cook spaghetti; drain, reserving 1/2 cup (125 mL) cooking water.

2. Return spaghetti to pot and keep warm.

3. Discard all but 2 tbsp (30 mL) of bacon fat in pan. Over medium-high heat, add cauliflower to pan; sauté until golden brown on its edges, about 8 to 10 minutes.

4. Toss in garlic, pepper and spaghetti to combine.

5. In bowl, whisk eggs with cheese.

6. Pour over spaghetti mixture. Remove from heat and toss, until thickened, to cook eggs.

7. Toss in bacon.

8. Transfer to serving bowl; garnish with parsley and more cheese.

Makes 4 servings

ITALIAN

lentil linguine
BOLOGNESE

INGREDIENTS

- [ ] 1 lb (450 g) linguini pasta, cooked and drained
- [ ] ½ cup (125 mL) grated Parmesan cheese (optional)

SAUCE

- [ ] 2 tbsp (30 mL) olive oil
- [ ] 1 small onion, diced
- [ ] 1 stalk celery, diced
- [ ] 1 carrot, diced
- [ ] 2 cloves garlic, minced
- [ ] 2 bay leaves
- [ ] 1 lb (450 g) dried red lentils
- [ ] 2 cans (each 14 oz / 398 mL) diced tomatoes, with juice
- [ ] 4 cups (1 L) low-sodium vegetable stock
- [ ] 1 tbsp (15 mL) tomato paste
- [ ] 2 tsp (10 mL) dried oregano, crumbled
- [ ] 2 tsp (10 mL) dried thyme, crumbled

This recipe uses a common combination of ingredients known as a 'mirepoix," which traditionally consists of one part carrot, one part celery and two parts onion, all diced about the same size. The combination is often used to bulk up a soup or a stew and, in this case, a sauce. Try using a frozen mirepoix, if it's available in your supermarket, to add all the extra flavour without all the chopping.

1. Sauce: In large saucepan over medium-high heat, warm oil. Sauté onion, celery and carrot until carrot is tender, 5 to 10 minutes.

2. Stir in garlic, bay leaves, lentils, tomatoes, vegetable stock, tomato paste, oregano and thyme. Reduce heat and simmer until lentils are tender, about 30 minutes.

3. Remove and discard bay leaves.

4. Divide linguini evenly among 6 servings dishes. Ladle sauce overtop. Sprinkle with cheese.

Makes 6 servings

VEGETARIAN

VEGAN

ITALIAN

VARIATION:
To keep this vegan, garnish with a drizzle of extra-virgin olive oil, instead of the cheese.

farmers' Market
FETTUCCINI

INGREDIENTS

- [ ] 2 tbsp (30 mL) olive oil
- [ ] 2 cloves garlic, minced (or ¹/₂ cup/125 mL diced garlic scapes)
- [ ] 1 cob corn kernels
- [ ] 1 zucchini, diced
- [ ] 1 small eggplant, cubed and well salted in a colander (see TIP below)
- [ ] 1 tomato, diced
- [ ] Pinch salt
- [ ] ¹/₄ cup (60 mL) butter
- [ ] ¹/₄ cup (60 mL) all-purpose flour
- [ ] 1 cup (250 mL) 2% milk
- [ ] ¹/₄ to ¹/₂ cup (60 to 125 mL) low-sodium chicken or vegetable stock
- [ ] ¹/₂ cup (125 mL) grated Parmesan cheese
- [ ] 4 oz (115 g) fettuccini pasta, cooked and drained
- [ ] ¹/₂ cup (125 mL) fresh basil, sliced + more for garnish
- [ ] Pepper to taste

This fresh and flavourful pasta dish is great any time of year, but especially great when your local market offers an abundant summer harvest. The sturdy strands of pasta stand up to a chunk of just about any vegetable, and the basic white sauce is perfect with produce from any season.

1. Rinse and pat dry salted eggplant.

2. In large saucepan over medium-high heat, warm oil. Sauté garlic, corn, zucchini, eggplant, tomato and salt until vegetables are tender.

3. With slotted spoon, transfer to bowl. Set aside.

4. In pan, melt butter. Whisk in flour until blended and smooth paste forms. Slowly whisk in milk until smooth and blended.

5. Whisk in chicken stock.

6. Stir in cheese and garlic mixture until heated through and cheese is melted.

7. Fold in fettuccini and basil. Garnish with basil and pepper.

Makes 4 servings

> **TIP:**
> Sprinkling a generous amount of salt over eggplant draws out any bitter flavour. Let the eggplant rest with lots of salt for a minimum of 5 to 10 minutes, and then rinse well to remove any bitter liquid before cooking.

VEGETARIAN

ITALIAN

Beef & Mushroom
STROGANOFF

$$
\begin{array}{}
\end{array}
$$

INGREDIENTS

- ☐ 2 tbsp (30 mL) olive oil
- ☐ 1 Vidalia onion, diced
- ☐ 2 cloves garlic, sliced
- ☐ 1 tsp (5 mL) paprika
- ☐ 3 cups (750 mL) chopped white, button, cremini and/or portobello mushrooms
- ☐ 2 tbsp (30 mL) red wine vinegar
- ☐ ²/₃ cup (150 mL) low-sodium beef stock
- ☐ 12 oz (340 g) partially frozen beef rump roast (see TIP below), cut in thin strips
- ☐ ²/₃ cup (150 mL) sour cream
- ☐ Sprigs parsley (optional)

This hearty dish is guaranteed to stick to your ribs. Lean beef, low-fat sour cream and meaty mushrooms make it taste indulgent without too many calories. Try serving this over a bed of egg noodles as a quick midweek meal.

1. In frying pan over medium-high heat, warm oil. Sauté onion just until golden, about 4 minutes.

2. Stir in garlic and paprika. Sauté for about 2 minutes.

3. Stir in mushrooms. Cook, stirring occasionally, for 5 to 10 minutes.

4. Stir in vinegar. Cook until about half of the liquid has been absorbed.

5. Stir in beef stock and beef. Reduce heat and simmer for 2 to 3 minutes.

6. Remove from heat. Stir in sour cream to coat.

7. Transfer to serving bowl; garnish with parsley (if using).

Makes 4 servings

ITALIAN

TIP:
Partially freezing the rump roast firms the meat, making it easier to thinly slice.

Creamy pesto pasta
with Chicken & Broccoli

INGREDIENTS

- [ ] 2 tbsp (30 mL) olive oil
- [ ] 4 boneless skinless chicken thighs or 1 boneless skinless chicken breast, thinly sliced
- [ ] 2 shallots, diced
- [ ] 2 cups (500 mL) fresh or thawed frozen broccoli florets
- [ ] 1/2 cup (125 mL) low-sodium chicken stock
- [ ] 1/3 cup (75 mL) store-bought pesto
- [ ] 4 oz (115 g) goat cheese, crumbled + more to garnish
- [ ] 8 oz (225 g) farfalle ('bowtie") pasta, cooked and drained
- [ ] Sprigs fresh parsley

Creamy pesto and goat cheese sauce falls into every nook and cranny of the pasta in this dish. It comes together in minutes, is nutritionally balanced and reminds us of home, making this a go-to staple for busy weeks.

1. In frying pan over medium-high heat, warm oil. Sauté chicken and shallots until chicken is cooked through and no longer pink in centre, 4 to 5 minutes.

2. Toss in broccoli. Sauté for 2 minutes.

3. Stir in chicken stock and pesto. Reduce heat and simmer, stirring occasionally, for 5 minutes.

4. Stir in cheese until melted and sauce is smooth.

5. Fold in farfalle. Cook, stirring, until heated through.

6. Transfer to serving bowl; garnish with more cheese and parsley.

Makes 2 to 4 servings

ITALIAN

Green Bean
& Red Potato Pesto Penne

INGREDIENTS

- [ ] 2 cups (500 mL) green beans sliced in 1-inch (2.5 cm) pieces
- [ ] 2 cups (500 mL) unpeeled small red potatoes, quartered
- [ ] 8 oz (225 g) penne pasta, cooked and drained, 1/2 cup (125 mL) cooking water reserved
- [ ] 1/2 cup (125 mL) store-bought pesto
- [ ] 2 tbsp (30 mL) toasted pine nuts, for garnish (optional)
- [ ] Sprigs fresh basil, for garnish (optional)

This is a delightful dish served hot or cold. You can serve it alongside a piping hot beef roast in the cooler months, or chill and pack it for an al fresco picnic in the summer.

1. In saucepan of boiling salted water, cook green beans for 3 minutes.

2. With slotted spoon, transfer to bowl.

3. Add potatoes to pot and cook until tender, about 10 minutes. Drain and transfer to bowl with beans.

4. In large saucepan over low heat, combine penne, pesto and reserved cooking water. Toss in bean mixture to coat.

5. Cook, stirring, until heated through, about 3 to 4 minutes.

6. Transfer to serving bowl. Garnish with pine nuts or basil (if using).

Makes 4 servings

VEGETARIAN

ITALIAN

sausage, kale &
Red Pepper Pasta

INGREDIENTS

- [ ] 2 tbsp (30 mL) olive oil
- [ ] 3 pork sausages, casings removed
- [ ] 2 or 3 shallots, minced
- [ ] 2 store-bought roasted red peppers, drained and chopped
- [ ] 1/4 tsp (1 mL) red pepper flakes
- [ ] 2 cans (each 14 oz/398 mL) store-bought fire-roasted tomatoes
- [ ] 2 cups (500 mL) chopped kale leaves
- [ ] 2 tbsp (30 mL) red wine vinegar
- [ ] About 1 tbsp (15 mL) sugar
- [ ] About 1/2 tsp (2 mL) salt
- [ ] 8 oz (225 g) penne pasta, cooked and drained
- [ ] 3 or 4 sprigs fresh parsley (optional)
- [ ] 1/2 cup (125 mL) grated Parmesan or grana Padano cheese

Spicy sausage, creamy roasted peppers and earthy kale taste so good that you'll want to double the recipe and have a second one stashed in the freezer. Try varying the pasta in this dish with different types of sturdy noodles — rigatoni, penne and egg noodles are all dense enough to carry this dish.

1. In large frying pan over medium-high heat, warm oil. Sauté sausages and shallots for 4 to 5 minutes.

2. Stir in red peppers and red pepper flakes. Sauté for 2 minutes.

3. Stir in tomatoes and kale. Reduce heat and simmer, stirring occasionally to break up tomatoes, for 5 to 10 minutes.

4. Stir in sugar and salt to taste. Toss in penne until coated. Cook, stirring, until heated through.

5. Transfer to serving bowl. Drizzle with vinegar and garnish with parsley (if using) and cheese.

Makes 4 servings

ITALIAN

veggie loaded
LASAGNA

INGREDIENTS

- [ ] 2 tbsp (30 mL) olive oil, divided
- [ ] 3 cloves garlic, minced
- [ ] 1/2 yellow onion, diced
- [ ] 1 cup (250 mL) chopped cremini mushrooms
- [ ] 1 zucchini, sliced
- [ ] 1 sweet pepper, chopped
- [ ] 1 tsp (5 mL) crumbled dried oregano
- [ ] 1 egg, beaten
- [ ] 1 can (22 oz/680 mL) tomato sauce
- [ ] 2 cups (500 mL) spinach, chopped
- [ ] 1 cup (250 mL) low-fat ricotta cheese
- [ ] 20 oven-ready lasagna pasta noodles
- [ ] 1 cup (250 mL) shredded mozzarella cheese

MAKE AHEAD:

If baking from frozen, preheat oven to 400°F (200°C). Place the tinfoil-wrapped frozen lasagna on a centre rack in the oven for about 45 to 60 minutes or until a knife inserted into the centre of the pan comes out warm. Remove the foil and bake for an additional 15 to 20 minutes to melt the cheese and reduce some of the sauce. Allow the lasagna to rest for another 15 to 20 minutes before slicing to serve.

Whipping up one of these is almost as easy as whipping up two, so prepare a pair, then cover and freeze the second one — assembled but uncooked — to have on hand for a healthy, hearty meal to pop into the oven during exam season. Try swapping out the vegetables with your own favourites such as eggplant, cauliflower, squash or broccoli.

1. Preheat oven to 375°F (190°C).

2. In large saucepan over medium heat, warm 1 tbsp (15 mL) of the oil. Sauté garlic, onion and mushrooms just until tender, about 3 to 4 minutes.

3. Stir in zucchini and sweet pepper. Sauté for 2 to 3 minutes.

4. Sprinkle with oregano. Remove from heat and set aside.

5. In bowl, stir together egg, spinach and ricotta cheese to combine and coat.

6. Brush remaining oil over bottom and sides of 13 x 9-inch (3.5 L) baking dish. Evenly spoon one-quarter of the tomato sauce in dish.

7. Arrange 4 lasagna noodles in single layer over tomato sauce, evenly top with half each of the egg mixture. Arrange another 4 lasagna noodles in single layer then evenly spoon one-quarter of the tomato sauce overtop followed by roughly half of the garlic mixture.

8. Arrange another 4 lasagna noodles overtop followed by an even spread of remaining egg mixture.

9. Arrange another layer of lasagna noodles over the egg mixture; followed by another 1/4 of the tomato sauce and remaining garlic mixture.

10. Layer final noodles, then evenly spoon remaining tomato sauce overtop and evenly sprinkle with mozzarella cheese.

11. Cover with foil and bake in oven for 35 to 40 minutes.

12. Uncover and bake until mozzarella cheese is melted and golden.

Makes 8 servings

VEGETARIAN

ITALIAN

Deep Dish
EGGPLANT PARM

VEGETARIAN

ITALIAN

INGREDIENTS

- ☐ 1/3 cup (75 mL) grated Parmesan cheese, divided
- ☐ 2 tbsp (30 mL) olive oil
- ☐ 1 egg
- ☐ 1 tbsp (15 mL) water
- ☐ 1 cup (250 mL) bread crumbs
- ☐ 1 tsp (5 mL) crumbled dried basil
- ☐ 1 tsp (5 mL) crumbled dried oregano
- ☐ 1 jar (22 oz/680 mL) store-bought low-sodium tomato sauce
- ☐ 1 large eggplant, sliced in 1/2-in (1 cm) rounds (about 8 slices)
- ☐ 1 cup (250 mL) shredded mozzarella cheese

Here's a lighter, crisp version of the traditionally deep-fried dish. Even if you think you don't like eggplant, you'll find it hard not to love it when it's bathed in your favourite tomato sauce, has crisp breaded topping and is oozing with melted cheese. Serve it between two slices of bread as a sandwich, next to a chunk of savoury protein or just on its own.

1. Preheat oven to 400°F (200°C).

2. Set aside 2 tbsp (30 mL) of the Parmesan cheese. Brush oil over rimmed baking sheet. Set aside.

3. In small bowl, whisk egg with water until blended.

4. In large dish, stir together bread crumbs, basil, oregano and remaining Parmesan cheese.

5. One at a time, dip eggplant rounds in egg mixture to coat all over. Dredge in bread crumb mixture to coat all over and transfer to baking sheet.

6. Bake in oven, turning once halfway through, until golden brown, 20 to 30 minutes.

7. Evenly spread about half of the tomato sauce over bottom of baking dish. Evenly arrange half of the eggplant rounds overtop and evenly sprinkle with half of the mozzarella cheese.

8. Repeat with remaining tomato sauce, eggplant rounds and mozzarella cheese. Sprinkle evenly with reserved Parmesan cheese.

9. Bake in 400°F (200°C) oven until sauce is bubbling and cheese is melted, about 15 minutes. Transfer pan to rack. Let stand for 5 minutes before serving.

Makes 4 servings

spaghetti Marinara
WITH TUNA & CHICKPEAS

INGREDIENTS

- [ ] 2 tbsp (30 mL) olive oil + more, for garnish
- [ ] 3 cloves garlic, diced
- [ ] Pinch red pepper flakes
- [ ] 1 can (19 oz/540 mL) diced tomatoes, with juice
- [ ] 1/2 tsp (2 mL) crumbled dried oregano
- [ ] 8 oz (225 g) spaghetti pasta, cooked and drained
- [ ] 1 can (6 oz/170 g) water-packed low-sodium chunk light tuna, drained
- [ ] 1 cup (250 mL) canned chickpeas, drained and rinsed
- [ ] 1/2 cup (125 mL) fresh basil leaves + more, for garnish

Pantry staples add up to a sum that is definitely better than its parts. Tomato sauce packed with cancer-preventing lycopene, fibre-rich chickpeas and tuna swimming in Omega-3s — it's ridiculous how healthy this meal is, even though it's almost entirely assembled with ingredients from boxes, jars and cans. Enjoy it with a side of steamed green vegetables such as broccoli or the Roasted Garlic Kale Caesar (page 42).

1. In large saucepan over medium-high heat, warm oil. Sauté garlic and red pepper flakes, stirring constantly until garlic is golden and fragrant, 2 to 3 minutes.

2. Stir in tomatoes and oregano. Reduce heat and simmer for 10 to 15 minutes.

3. Add pasta. Toss mixture well to coat the pasta.

4. Stir in tuna, chickpeas and basil. Simmer until heated through and sauce is thickened, 4 to 6 minutes.

5. Transfer to serving bowl. Garnish with basil and drizzle with oil.

Makes 4 servings

ITALIAN

DELICIOUS PIZZAS

INGREDIENTS

CRUST

- [ ] 1 package active dry yeast
- [ ] 3 1/2 cups (875 mL) all-purpose or bread flour
- [ ] 2 tsp (10 mL) salt
- [ ] 1 tsp (5 mL) sugar
- [ ] 1 1/2 cups (375 mL) warm water
- [ ] 3 tbsp (45 mL) olive oil, divided

VEGETARIAN

VEGAN

ITALIAN

TIPS:
Many supermarkets sell fresh pizza dough either refrigerated or frozen. If this is an easier option, simply let purchased dough come to room temperature before rolling.
To really save time, you can also substitute large pitas or tortillas for the crust.

MAKE AHEAD:
To save unbaked crust for later, wrap tightly in plastic wrap and place in a resealable freezer bag. Refrigerate for up to 3 to 5 days or freeze for later use.

If there is a single most-loved food in the world, it might just be pizza. A salty, chewy and moist crust topped with delicious sauce and your favourite toppings always has the makings of a crowd-pleaser. It's quick and easy to make — and so versatile!

1. In large bowl, whisk yeast, flour, salt and sugar. With fork, stir in water and 2 tbsp (30 mL) of the oil until dough comes together in soft smooth (not sticky) ball.

2. Transfer to lightly floured surface. With clean and dry hands knead into firm ball.

3. Using the remaining oil, grease a clean bowl and place the ball of dough inside. Cover with plastic wrap or tea towel and let rise in warm draft-free place for 1 hour.

4. Transfer to lightly floured work surface. Cut dough into 2 roughly equal sized balls to make 2 14-inch (35 cm) pizzas or 4 pieces for 4 smaller 6-inch (15 cm) pizzas.

5. Form dough into balls. One at a time, flatten each into round. Sprinkle with flour and roll into crust of preferred size.

6. Transfer to rimless baking sheet(s).

Makes 2 14-inch (35 cm) crusts or 4 6-inch (15 cm) crusts

BBQ Chicken Pizza

INGREDIENTS

- [ ] One 14-inch (35 cm) pizza crust (see recipe, page 128)
- [ ] ³/₄ cup (375 mL) store-bought BBQ sauce, divided
- [ ] 1 cup (250 mL) shredded cooked chicken
- [ ] 1 ¹/₂ cups (375 mL) broccoli florets
- [ ] 1 cup (250 mL) shredded mozzarella cheese
- [ ] 1 cup (250 mL) shredded cheddar cheese
- [ ] ¹/₂ cup (125 mL) red onion rings
- [ ] ¹/₂ cup (125 mL) chopped fresh cilantro leaves

1. Preheat oven to 450°F (230°C).

2. Place the pizza crust on a baking sheet and spread crust with about three-quarters of the BBQ sauce. Set aside.

3. In small bowl, toss chicken with remaining BBQ sauce to coat. Arrange evenly over crust, then top with broccoli, mozzarella cheese, cheddar cheese and onion.

4. Bake in oven until cheese is melted and crust is browned, 8 to 12 minutes. Top with cilantro.

ITALIAN

Cherry Tomato Pizza
WITH LEMONY ARUGULA

INGREDIENTS

- [ ] One 14-inch (35 cm) pizza crust (see recipe, page 128)
- [ ] 4 tbsp (60 mL) olive oil, divided
- [ ] 1 cup (250 mL) cherry tomatoes, halved
- [ ] $^1/_2$ cup (125 mL) crumbled goat cheese
- [ ] $^1/_2$ cup (125 mL) fresh basil leaves
- [ ] 2 tbsp (30 mL) lemon juice
- [ ] 1 tbsp (15 mL) liquid honey
- [ ] 2 cups (250 mL) arugula
- [ ] Pepper to taste

1. Preheat oven to 450°F (230°C).

2. Place the pizza crust on a baking sheet and brush the crust with 2 tbsp (30 mL) of the oil.

3. Top with tomatoes, cheese and basil.

4. Bake in oven until cheese is melted and crust is browned, 8 to 12 minutes.

5. Meanwhile, in bowl, whisk remaining oil, lemon juice and honey; toss in arugula to coat.

6. Arrange arugula over pizza. Sprinkle with pepper.

VEGETARIAN

ITALIAN

Roma Tomato, Basil
& Balsamic Pizza

INGREDIENTS

- [ ] One 14-inch (35 cm) pizza crust (see recipe, page 128)
- [ ] ¼ cup (60 mL) olive oil
- [ ] 3 cloves garlic, thinly sliced
- [ ] 2 small Roma tomatoes, thinly sliced
- [ ] 2 cups (500 mL) shredded mozzarella cheese
- [ ] ½ cup (125 mL) fresh basil leaves
- [ ] ½ cup (125 mL) balsamic vinegar
- [ ] Pepper to taste

1. Preheat oven to 450°F (230°C).

2. Place the pizza crust on a baking sheet and spread the olive oil evenly over the crust; evenly top with garlic, tomatoes, cheese and basil.

3. Bake in oven until cheese is melted and crust is browned, 8 to 12 minutes.

4. Meanwhile, in small saucepan over medium heat, simmer vinegar until thickened and syrupy, 8 to 10 minutes. Use this as a glaze and drizzle over pizza; sprinkle with pepper.

> **! MAKE AHEAD:**
> Refrigerate vinegar reduction in airtight container for up to 6 months or even longer.

VEGETARIAN

ITALIAN

The Big Greek
PIZZA

INGREDIENTS

- [ ] One 14-inch (35 cm) pizza crust (see recipe, page 128)
- [ ] ³/₄ cup (175 mL) store-bought pizza sauce
- [ ] 1 ¹/₂ cups (375 mL) shredded mozzarella cheese
- [ ] 1 cup (250 mL) diced tomatoes
- [ ] ¹/₂ cup (125 mL) sliced kalamata olives
- [ ] ¹/₂ cup (125 mL) crumbled feta cheese
- [ ] 1 tbsp (15 mL) crumbled dried oregano

1. Preheat oven to 450°F (230°C).

2. Place the pizza crust on a baking sheet and spread crust with pizza sauce. Evenly top with mozzarella cheese, tomatoes, olives, feta cheese and oregano.

3. Bake in oven until cheese is melted and crust is browned, 8 to 12 minutes.

VEGETARIAN

ITALIAN

spinach, Bacon &
Fried Egg Breakfast Pizza

INGREDIENTS

- [ ] One 14-inch (35 cm) pizza crust (see recipe, page 128)
- [ ] 1/4 cup (60 mL) olive oil
- [ ] 2 cups (500 mL) loosely packed baby spinach
- [ ] 1 1/2 cups (375 mL) shredded mozzarella cheese
- [ ] 1/4 cup (60 mL) grated Parmesan cheese
- [ ] 6 slices bacon, chopped and cooked, 2 tsp (10 mL) bacon fat reserved in pan
- [ ] 3 eggs
- [ ] Pepper to taste

1. Preheat oven to 450°F (230°C).

2. Place the pizza crust on a baking sheet and spread the olive oil evenly over the crust. Evenly top with spinach, mozzarella cheese, Parmesan cheese and bacon.

3. Bake in oven until cheese is melted and crust is browned, 8 to 12 minutes.

4. Meanwhile, in pan over medium heat, warm reserved bacon fat. Fry eggs over easy (whites are set, but yolks are runny).

5. With spatula, transfer to pizza, slicing through runny yolks. Sprinkle with pepper.

ITALIAN

Hot Hawaiian
PIZZA

INGREDIENTS

- [ ] One 14-inch (35 cm) pizza crust (see recipe, page 128)
- [ ] ³/₄ cup (375 mL) store-bought pizza sauce
- [ ] 2 cups (500 mL) shredded mozzarella cheese
- [ ] 1 cup (250 mL) pineapple chunks
- [ ] 5 or 6 thin slices low-sodium deli ham
- [ ] ¹/₄ cup (60 mL) pickled jalapeño peppers

1. Preheat oven to 450°F (230°C).

2. Place the pizza crust on a baking sheet and cover with pizza sauce. Evenly top with cheese, pineapple, ham and jalapeño.

3. Bake in oven until cheese is melted and crust is browned, 8 to 12 minutes.

ITALIAN

farmers' Market Veggie
PIZZA

INGREDIENTS

- [ ] One 14-inch (35 cm) pizza crust (see recipe, page 128)
- [ ] ³/₄ cup (375 mL) store-bought pizza sauce
- [ ] 2 cups (500 mL) shredded mozzarella cheese
- [ ] 1 sweet pepper, sliced in rings
- [ ] 1 Roma tomato, diced
- [ ] 2 slices red onion, broken in rings
- [ ] ¹/₂ cup (125 mL) sliced white mushrooms

1. Preheat oven to 450°F (230°C).

2. Place pizza crust on a baking sheet and spread crust with pizza sauce. Evenly top with cheese, sweet pepper, tomato, onion and mushrooms.

3. Bake in oven until cheese is melted and crust is browned, 8 to 12 minutes.

VEGETARIAN

ITALIAN

Broccoli, Bacon & pea
MACARONI AND CHEESE

INGREDIENTS

- [ ] 2 tbsp (30 mL) butter
- [ ] 1 clove garlic, pressed
- [ ] $1/2$ tsp (2 mL) white pepper
- [ ] $1/2$ tsp (2 mL) chili powder
- [ ] 2 cups (500 mL) 1 or 2% milk
- [ ] 8 oz (225 g) reduced-sodium cream cheese
- [ ] 2 cups (500 mL) shredded cheddar cheese + more for garnish (optional)
- [ ] 3 cups (750 mL) macaroni pasta, cooked and drained
- [ ] 4 slices bacon, cooked and chopped, divided
- [ ] 1 cup (250 mL) fresh or thawed frozen broccoli florets
- [ ] $1/2$ cup (125 mL) fresh or thawed frozen peas

Super-easy mac and cheese doesn't need to come from a box. This one is kid-friendly, adult-approved and perfect for rainy days.

1. In large saucepan over medium-high heat, melt butter. Sauté garlic, white pepper and chili powder for about 1 minute.

2. Reduce heat to medium, stir in milk and bring to a simmer.

3. Stir in cream cheese until blended and smooth. Stir in cheddar cheese. Cook, stirring constantly, until melted and blended.

4. Stir in macaroni, three-quarters of the bacon, broccoli and peas; simmer, stirring, until heated through.

5. Transfer to serving bowl; garnish with remaining bacon and cheddar cheese (if using).

Makes 4 servings

ITALIAN

VARIATION:
Preheat oven to 400°F (200°C). Assemble macaroni mixture, using all of the bacon and omitting garnish, and scrape into greased baking dish. In small bowl with fork, stir together 1/2 cup (125 mL) panko or Italian-seasoned bread crumbs and 2 tbsp (30 mL) melted butter to coat; evenly sprinkle over macaroni mixture. Bake in oven until topping is golden and cheese is bubbling, about 15 minutes.

MAKE AHEAD:
Cover and refrigerate for up to 4 days, or freeze for up to 1 month.

Baja Fish Tacos

This Californian-Mexican fusion is a food-truck favourite. Smoky tender fish, bright and creamy slaw and earthy tortillas, this recipe feels like summer but will become a staple year-round.

INGREDIENTS

- [ ] ¹/₂ red onion, thinly sliced
- [ ] 1 cup (250 mL) red wine vinegar
- [ ] ¹/₄ cup (60 mL) olive oil
- [ ] 1 ¹/₂ tsp (7 mL) chili powder
- [ ] 1 ¹/₂ tsp (7 mL) ground cumin
- [ ] 1 ¹/₂ tsp (7 mL) crumbled dried oregano
- [ ] 1 lb (450 g) tilapia or other white fish fillets
- [ ] 8 flour tortillas, toasted (see TIP below)
- [ ] 2 limes, cut in wedges

SLAW

- [ ] 2 carrots, grated
- [ ] 1 small red cabbage, grated
- [ ] 1 jalapeño pepper, seeded and diced
- [ ] ¹/₄ cup (60 mL) lightly packed fresh cilantro leaves + extra, for garnish

CREMA

- [ ] ¹/₃ cup (75 mL) mayonnaise
- [ ] ¹/₄ cup (60 mL) milk

1. In small bowl cover red onion with vinegar; set aside to marinate.

2. In another small bowl, whisk oil, chili powder, cumin and oregano.

3. Transfer to large resealable plastic bag along with tilapia. Use your hands to gently move the fish around inside the bag to coat it in the oil and spices.

4. Set aside at room temperature for 15 minutes or so, while preparing the veggie slaw and crema.

5. Slaw: In large bowl, toss together carrots, cabbage, jalapeño and cilantro.

6. Crema: In small bowl, whisk mayonnaise with milk; pour about half over slaw, tossing to coat. Set aside remaining half.

7. In a non-stick pan over medium heat, gently toast the tortillas, one at a time for about 1 minute per tortilla, flipping sides about halfway through. Wrap the heated tortillas in a clean tea towel inside a covered dish to keep them warm.

8. With tongs, transfer tilapia to preheated non-stick saucepan over medium-high heat. Fry just until opaque, about 4 minutes.

9. With spatula, turn over. Cook, breaking up fillets, for 2 minutes or until desired doneness.

10. Divide slaw and tilapia evenly among tacos; top with spoonful of crema and garnish with cilantro. Serve with lime wedges on side.

Makes 4 servings

TIP:

Toast tortillas in dry non-stick saucepan or frying pan over medium-heat, turning once halfway through, for about 1 minute. Wrap in tea towel and place in covered dish to keep warm until ready to use.

VARIATION:

Experiment with fun additions such as pickled hot peppers and shredded sharp cheddar cheese, or fresh dill instead of cilantro.

MEXICAN

Slow Cooker Chipotle
Beef Tacos

INGREDIENTS

- [ ] 1 tsp (5 mL) chili powder
- [ ] 1 tsp (5 mL) ground cumin
- [ ] 1/2 tsp (2 mL) smoked paprika
- [ ] 2 lb (900 g) beef chuck roast
- [ ] 2 tbsp (30 mL) olive oil
- [ ] 1 cup (250 mL) beef stock
- [ ] 1 chipotle pepper in adobo sauce
- [ ] 1 tbsp (15 mL) tomato paste
- [ ] 1 large red onion, diced
- [ ] 8 corn tortillas, warmed (see TIP below)
- [ ] 1 cup (250 mL) sour cream or Greek yogurt
- [ ] 1 cup (250 mL) store-bought salsa

SLAW

- [ ] 2 tbsp (30 mL) lime juice
- [ ] 1 tbsp (15 mL) liquid honey
- [ ] 1/2 tsp (2 mL) salt
- [ ] 2 cups (500 mL) shredded cabbage
- [ ] 1 cup (250 mL) shredded carrot
- [ ] 1/2 cup (125 mL) chopped fresh cilantro

Smoky, tangy beef soaked in delicious sauce contrasts nicely with the fresh crunch of a vegetable slaw. Great as a taco, this filling is perfect in a burrito bowl, fajita or a salad.

1. In small bowl, mix chili powder, cumin and paprika; rub all over beef to coat.

2. In large frying pan over medium-high heat, warm oil; sear beef, 2 to 3 minutes per side. The goal here is to get a nice caramelization on the outside of the meat, almost forming a crust. Then transfer to slow cooker.

3. Add beef stock to pan and cook, scraping up brown bits from bottom of pan. Stir in chipotle pepper and tomato paste.

4. Pour into slow cooker. Arrange onion overtop. Cover and cook on low until beef is tender and falling apart, 6 to 8 hours.

5. With tongs, transfer beef to cutting board. With two forks, pull apart.

6. Return to slow cooker. Cook, uncovered, until cooking liquid is thickened into gravy.

7. Slaw: In large bowl, whisk lime juice, honey and salt. Toss in cabbage, carrot and cilantro to coat.

8. Divide beef, gravy and slaw evenly among tortillas; serve with sour cream and salsa on side.

Makes 4 servings of 2 tacos each

TIPS:
The best way to sear beef is to leave it alone! Moving it around the pan and fussing with it will not develop the smoky flavour that you want in this dish.
Cover and microwave tortillas for 30 to 60 seconds to warm through.

Slow Cooker Sriracha
Pork Tacos w/ Pineapple Salsa

INGREDIENTS

- [ ] 1 tsp (5 mL) canola oil
- [ ] 2 lb (900 g) pork shoulder roast
- [ ] 2 cloves garlic, minced or pressed
- [ ] ¹/₂ cup (125 mL) store-bought barbecue sauce
- [ ] ¹/₂ cup (125 mL) reserved pineapple juice from Salsa, below
- [ ] ¹/₄ cup (60 mL) apple cider vinegar
- [ ] ¹/₂ cup (125 mL) diced onion
- [ ] 2 tbsp (30 mL) packed brown sugar
- [ ] 1 tbsp (15 mL) Sriracha sauce
- [ ] 1 tsp (5 mL) ground cumin
- [ ] 1 avocado, cubed
- [ ] 8 flour tortillas, warmed (see TIP below)

SALSA

- [ ] 1 jalapeño pepper, seeded and diced
- [ ] ¹/₂ avocado, chopped
- [ ] 1 can (14 oz/398 mL) pineapple chunks, drained and juice reserved
- [ ] ¹/₄ cup (60 mL) diced red onion
- [ ] ¹/₄ cup (60 mL) fresh cilantro leaves, chopped + extra for garnish
- [ ] 2 tsp (10 mL) lime juice
- [ ] Salt to taste

This recipe doubles up easily for a party or to freeze a batch for a busy time. With a slow cooker, you can make lots without heating up your whole apartment in the summer. The best part, though, is that all you need to do is dump in the ingredients, then come home hours later to the aroma of spicy meaty goodness.

1. Pour oil into slow cooker. Place pork on top. Add garlic, barbecue sauce, pineapple juice, vinegar, onion, brown sugar, Sriracha sauce and cumin, stirring to combine.

2. Cook on high for 4 to 6 hours.

3. With tongs, transfer pork to cutting board. With two forks, shred pork.

4. Return the pork to the slow cooker and leave uncovered on warm to soak up the juices left behind while you prepare the salsa.

5. Salsa: In large bowl, toss together jalapeño, avocado, pineapple, onion, cilantro, lime juice and salt.

6. Divide pork, salsa and avocado evenly among tortillas; garnish with cilantro.

Makes 4 servings

TIP:
To warm tortillas, arrange on rimmed baking sheet and bake in 250°F (120°C) oven for 15 minutes or wrap with damp paper towel and microwave for 30 to 60 seconds.

$$

MEXICAN

sweet potato &
BLACK BEAN BURRITOS

INGREDIENTS

- [ ] 2 unpeeled sweet potatoes
- [ ] 6 large whole-grain flour tortillas

SAUCE

- [ ] 2 cloves garlic, minced
- [ ] 1 jalapeño pepper, seeded and minced
- [ ] 1/4 red onion, diced
- [ ] 1 can (14 oz/398 mL) black beans, drained and rinsed
- [ ] 2 tbsp (30 mL) lime juice
- [ ] 1 tbsp (15 mL) olive oil
- [ ] 1 tbsp (15 mL) chili powder
- [ ] 1/2 tsp (2 mL) ground cumin
- [ ] 2 cups (500 mL) store-bought salsa
- [ ] 1/4 cup (60 mL) chopped fresh cilantro

VARIATIONS:

If reheating burrito from frozen, remove foil and microwave on high until heated through, 2 to 3 minutes. Top with 1/4 cup (60 mL) shredded cheddar or Monterey Jack cheese and microwave for another minute. Top with additional avocado, sour cream and/or beans.

MAKE AHEAD:

Wrap each burrito in foil and crimp the edges. Freeze foil-wrapped burritos in an airtight resealable plastic bag for up to 2 months.

I call these "emergency burritos" because they make a delicious, healthy dinner or lunch in only 2 or 3 minutes from the freezer. Sweet Potatoes and black beans complement each other nicely in a base of smoky Tex-Mex spices. Wrapped snugly in whole-grain tortillas, these earn bonus marks for being portable.

1. With fork, pierce sweet potatoes all over. Microwave on high until tender, about 5 minutes, rotating halfway through. Set aside. Let cool enough to handle.

2. Sauce: In food processor, purée garlic, jalapeño, onion, beans, lime juice, oil, chili powder and cumin until blended and smooth.

3. Transfer to large non-stick frying pan over medium-high heat. Cook, stirring constantly, until thickened, about 5 minutes.

4. Slice sweet potato into cubes.

5. From foil, cut 6 squares, each slightly larger than tortilla. Lay 1 tortilla on each.

6. Top each tortilla with 1/6 of the sweet potato, 1/6 of the sauce and about 1/3 cup (75 mL) of the salsa. Sprinkle with cilantro.

7. Roll each tortilla into burrito and top with 1/4 cup (60 mL) shredded cheddar or Monterey Jack cheese.

8. Bake in a 400°F (200°C) oven for 5 to10 minutes.

9. Top with additional avocado, sour cream and/or beans.

Makes 6 burritos

Mexican Quinoa & Beans

INGREDIENTS

- [ ] 1 tbsp (15 mL) olive oil
- [ ] 2 cloves garlic, minced
- [ ] ¼ jalapeño pepper, seeded and minced
- [ ] ¼ red onion, diced
- [ ] 1 can (14 oz / 398 mL) black beans, drained and rinsed
- [ ] 1 can (14 oz / 398 mL) tomatoes with juice
- [ ] 1 cup (250 mL) uncooked quinoa
- [ ] 1 cup (250 mL) vegetable stock
- [ ] 1 cup (250 mL) corn kernels
- [ ] 1 tbsp (15 mL) chili powder
- [ ] ½ tsp (2 mL) ground cumin
- [ ] 1 sweet pepper, diced
- [ ] 1 avocado, diced
- [ ] 2 tbsp (30 mL) chopped fresh cilantro
- [ ] 2 tbsp (30 mL) lime juice

The nutty taste of quinoa is given a piquant flavour boost with Mexican staples such as hot jalapeño, tangy lime juice and aromatic garlic. You can use this as a filling for burritos, enjoy it cold as a salad, or serve it alongside additional protein such as tofu or a fried egg. Adjust the spices to your own taste, and add your favorite veggies, if you like, to boost nutrition.

1. In large saucepan over medium-high heat, warm oil. Sauté garlic, jalapeño and onion for about 2 minutes.

2. Stir in beans, tomatoes, quinoa, vegetable stock, corn, chili powder and cumin and bring to a boil. Reduce heat and simmer until quinoa is tender and grains are edged with white, about 15 minutes.

3. Stir in red pepper, avocado, cilantro and lime juice.

Makes 4 servings

> **VARIATION:**
> Add more vegetables, such as butternut squash or sweet potato, and/or more protein, such as tofu, cheddar or Monterey Jack cheese, to make this a balanced meal.

VEGETARIAN

VEGAN

MEXICAN

Tortilla, Tomato, Black Bean & Corn Lasagna

INGREDIENTS

- [ ] 2 tbsp (30 mL) canola oil, divided
- [ ] 2 lb (900 g) extra-lean ground chicken
- [ ] ½ cup (125 mL) thinly sliced red onion
- [ ] 2 tbsp (30 mL) chili powder
- [ ] 1 can (14 oz/398 mL) black beans, drained and rinsed
- [ ] 1 can (14 oz/398 mL) fire-roasted tomatoes, with juice
- [ ] 1 cup (250 mL) thawed frozen corn
- [ ] 8 to 10 large flour tortillas, quartered
- [ ] 2½ cups (625 mL) shredded cheddar or Monterey Jack cheese
- [ ] 1 cup (250 mL) sour cream or Greek yogurt
- [ ] 2 green onions, thinly sliced

A Mexican-inspired lasagna that delivers the yummy flavour of a Mexican feast baked in one easy dish. Entirely made from whole foods, this lasagna is a complete meal containing healthful and nutritious ingredients that are kid-friendly, as well. Try using gluten-free tortillas to please a crowd.

1. Preheat oven to 425°F (220°C).

2. In large non-stick saucepan, warm 1 tbsp (15 mL) of the oil. Sauté chicken, onion and chili powder, breaking up chicken, until chicken is cooked through and no longer pink in centre, about 5 minutes.

3. Stir in beans, tomatoes and corn. Cook, stirring, until heated through.

4. Brush remaining oil over bottom of baking dish. Evenly arrange one-third of the tortillas in single layer on bottom. Evenly top with one-third of the chicken mixture and one-third of the cheese.

5. Repeat twice to make 3 layers of tortillas, chicken mixture and cheese. Bake in oven for 15 to 20 minutes.

6. Divide evenly among 4 serving bowls; top each with spoonful of sour cream and garnish with green onions.

Makes 4 servings

MEXICAN

Easy Huevos Rancheros

INGREDIENTS

- [ ] 2 tbsp (30 mL) olive oil, divided
- [ ] 2 cloves garlic, minced
- [ ] 1 jalapeño pepper, seeded and minced
- [ ] 1/2 sweet red pepper, diced
- [ ] 1/4 red onion, diced
- [ ] 1 cup (250 mL) black beans, drained and rinsed
- [ ] 1/2 tsp (2 mL) ground cumin
- [ ] 4 corn tortillas, warmed (see TIP below)
- [ ] 4 eggs
- [ ] 1 tomato, diced
- [ ] 1/4 cup (60 mL) crumbled feta cheese
- [ ] 2 tbsp (30 mL) chopped fresh cilantro
- [ ] 2 tbsp (30 mL) lime juice

Salted, spiced and savoury eggs are a tried-and-true brunch favourite, but they also make a delicious balanced supper. A crispy tortilla, seasoned beans and the fresh tomato, cilantro and zesty lime are excellent complements . You can serve these with a wedge or two of fresh avocado and a simple green salad.

1. In large saucepan over medium-high heat, warm 1 tbsp (15 mL) of the oil. Sauté garlic, jalapeño, red pepper, onion, beans and cumin for 4 to 5 minutes.

2. Place 1 tortilla on each serving plate. Divide garlic mixture evenly among tortillas.

3. To pan, add remaining oil. Crack eggs into pan and quickly fry over easy (whites are set, but yolks are runny).

4. With spatula, transfer 1 egg to each tortilla. Top each with one-quarter of the tomato and one quarter of the cheese; sprinkle with cilantro and drizzle with lime juice.

Makes 4 servings

> **TIP:**
> Warm tortillas in 350°F (180°C) oven for 4 to 5 minutes.
>
> **VARIATION:**
> Make this a vegan dish by replacing eggs with 1 cup (250 mL) crumbled vegan chorizo sausage, and using diced avocado instead of cheese.

VEGETARIAN

VEGAN

MEXICAN

Black Bean floutas &
Charred Tomato Salsa

INGREDIENTS

- ☐ 3 unpeeled cloves garlic
- ☐ 1 can (14 oz/398 mL) black beans, drained and rinsed
- ☐ 1 cup (250 mL) vegetable or chicken stock
- ☐ 1 tsp (5 mL) chili powder
- ☐ $^1/_2$ tsp (2 mL) ground cumin
- ☐ $^1/_4$ cup (60 mL) lime juice
- ☐ $^1/_4$ cup (60 mL) fresh cilantro, chopped + extra, for garnish
- ☐ 8 flour tortillas
- ☐ 2 cups (500 mL) shredded Monterey Jack cheese
- ☐ Salt and pepper to taste

SALSA

- ☐ 3 Roma tomatoes
- ☐ 1 yellow onion
- ☐ 1 jalapeño pepper
- ☐ 3 unpeeled cloves garlic
- ☐ $^1/_4$ cup (60 mL) lime juice
- ☐ Salt to taste

Black beans are spiced and puréed until creamy, wrapped inside a tortilla and topped with a smoky salsa with just the right amount of heat. You can also use this bean filling as a dip for corn chips, as a spread on sandwiches or as a topping for baked sweet potatoes.

1. Preheat oven to 450°F (230°C).

2. Smash 3 cloves of garlic, peel off and discard skin; transfer to saucepan over medium-high heat along with beans, vegetable stock, chili powder and cumin and bring to a gentle simmer.

3. Cook, stirring occasionally, for 10 to 15 minutes. Remove from heat and let cool.

4. Salsa: On rimmed baking sheet, arrange tomatoes, onion and jalapeño. Transfer to top rack in oven and broil, turning once and tossing in remaining garlic halfway through, until skins are charred, about 10 minutes.

5. Remove from heat. Let cool enough to handle. Peel off and discard skins

6. Transfer to food processor or blender. Add lime juice and salt and purée until blended and smooth. Set aside.

7. In food processor or blender, purée bean mixture, lime juice and cilantro until blended and smooth.

8. Lay tortillas flat on work surface. On each, spread about one-eighth of the bean mixture and one-quarter of the cheese, then tightly roll up and transfer, seam side down, to rimmed baking sheet.

9. Bake in oven until filling is heated through and cheese is melted, 5 to 8 minutes.

10. Transfer each to serving plate, spoon salsa overtop and garnish with cilantro to complete flouta.

Makes 4 servings

MAKE AHEAD:
Wrap assembled floutas without salsa in plastic wrap and refrigerate for up to 4 days; bake in 350°F (175°C) oven for 20 to 25 minutes to reheat.
This delicious and healthful salsa is a great condiment to have on hand. Double the recipe (if you love it as much as I do), then transfer the extra to an airtight container and refrigerate for up to 5 days.

Chicken, Black Bean &
Rice Enchiladas

INGREDIENTS

SAUCE

- ☐ 2 tbsp (30 mL) olive oil
- ☐ 2 tbsp (30 mL) all-purpose flour
- ☐ 1 can (10 oz/284 mL) tomato paste
- ☐ 2 cups (250 mL) reduced-sodium chicken stock
- ☐ 1/4 cup (60 mL) chili powder
- ☐ 1 tsp (5 mL) crumbled dried oregano
- ☐ 1 tsp (5 mL) ground cumin

ENCHILADAS

- ☐ 1 cup (250 mL) shredded cooked chicken
- ☐ 1 cup (250 mL) black beans, drained and rinsed
- ☐ 1 cup (250 mL) cooked rice, cooled
- ☐ 1/2 cup (125 mL) thinly sliced red onion
- ☐ 2 tbsp (30mL) canola oil
- ☐ 8-10 corn tortillas
- ☐ 1 cup (250 mL) shredded colby or Monterey Jack cheese
- ☐ 1/2 cup (125 mL) chopped fresh cilantro

Easy enchilada sauce is miles better than the canned stuff, and this recipe transforms leftover chicken and rice into an entirely new meal.

1. Sauce: In saucepan over medium-high heat, warm oil. Stir in flour to make a paste and cook, stirring, for about 1 minute.

2. Preheat oven to 375°F (190°C).

3. Stir in tomato paste, chicken stock, chili powder, oregano and cumin until blended. Reduce heat to medium and simmer, stirring occasionally, until thickened.

4. In bowl, toss together chicken, beans, rice and onion; set aside.

5. In large frying pan over medium-high heat, warm oil. One at a time, quickly fry tortillas, turning once, just until heated through (do not fry until crisp).

6. Evenly spoon 1 cup (250 mL) sauce over bottom of baking dish. Set aside.

7. Lay tortillas flat on work surface; evenly spread one-third cup of the chicken mixture over each, then tightly roll and transfer, seam side down, into baking dish.

8. Evenly pour sauce overtop. Sprinkle cheese in line across centre, perpendicular to the enchiladas.

9. Bake in oven until cheese is bubbling and golden, about 20 minutes. Garnish with cilantro.

Makes 4 servings

MEXICAN

Quinoa, Bean &
Chickpea Chili

INGREDIENTS

- [ ] 2 tbsp (30 mL) olive oil
- [ ] 4 cloves garlic, minced
- [ ] 2 small red onions, diced
- [ ] 1 sweet green pepper, diced
- [ ] 1 jalapeño pepper, seeded and minced
- [ ] 2 tbsp (30 mL) chili powder
- [ ] 1 tsp (5 mL) ground cumin
- [ ] 1 tsp (5 mL) smoked paprika
- [ ] 1 can (14 oz/398 mL) diced tomatoes, with juice
- [ ] 1 can (14 oz/398 mL) low-sodium tomato sauce
- [ ] 3 cups (750 mL) low-sodium vegetable stock
- [ ] 1 cup (250 mL) quinoa, rinsed
- [ ] 1 can (14 oz/398 mL) chickpeas, drained and rinsed
- [ ] 1 can (14 oz/398 mL) kidney beans, drained and rinsed
- [ ] 2 tbsp (30 mL) packed brown sugar
- [ ] 2 tbsp (30 mL) lime juice
- [ ] 2 cups (500 mL) shredded old cheddar cheese (optional)
- [ ] 1/2 cup (125 mL) chopped fresh cilantro

Chili is a great meal to make for meal prep on Sundays. A nice alternative to this dish is throwing all of the ingredients into a slow cooker and cooking on low for 4 to 6 hours.

1. In large saucepan over medium-high heat, warm oil. Sauté garlic, onions, green pepper and jalapeño until turning translucent and golden at the edges, 4 to 5 minutes.

2. Stir in chili powder, cumin and paprika. Sauté until fragrant, about 30 seconds.

3. Stir in tomatoes, tomato sauce, vegetable stock and quinoa. Cover, reduce heat and simmer until quinoa is tender and each grain is edged with white, about 15 minutes.

4. Stir in chickpeas, beans, brown sugar and lime juice. Simmer until heated through, about 5 minutes.

5. Transfer to serving bowl; garnish with cheese and cilantro.

Makes 6 servings

VEGETARIAN

VEGAN

TEX-MEX

Mexican stewed
Zucchini & Tomato

INGREDIENTS

- [ ] 1 tbsp (15 mL) olive oil
- [ ] 2 cloves garlic, minced
- [ ] 1/2 small onion, sliced
- [ ] 4 zucchini, sliced into 1/4-inch (5 cm) rounds
- [ ] 1 can (14 oz/398 mL) diced tomatoes, with juice
- [ ] 1/4 cup (60 mL) crumbled feta cheese
- [ ] 2 tbsp (30 mL) chopped fresh cilantro

This super-healthy Mexican side is delicious on its own or as a side for other Mexican dishes.

1. In large frying pan over medium-high heat, warm oil. Sauté garlic and onion for about 2 minutes.

2. Stir in zucchini and tomatoes. Reduce heat and simmer until zucchini is tender, 5 to 10 minutes.

3. Sprinkle cheese overtop. Cover and cook until cheese is melted, about 2 minutes.

4. Garnish with cilantro.

Makes 4 servings

VEGETARIAN

MEXICAN

Quinoa, Black Bean
Salsa & Cheddar Stuffed Red Peppers

INGREDIENTS

- [ ] 2 cups (500 mL) store-bought low-sodium salsa
- [ ] 2 tbsp (30 mL) olive oil, divided
- [ ] 1 ½ cups (375 mL) cooked quinoa
- [ ] 1 cup (250 mL) black beans, drained and rinsed
- [ ] 4 large sweet red peppers
- [ ] 1 cup (250 mL) shredded old cheddar cheese
- [ ] ¼ cup (60 mL) chopped fresh cilantro

Stuffed peppers can be found in many global cuisines, but these Mexican-inspired peppers are as fresh and spicy as they are satisfying and nutritious. Try serving with some pickled jalapeños to turn up the heat.

1. Preheat oven to 375°F (190°C).

2. In large frying pan over medium-high heat, stir together salsa and 1 tbsp (15 mL) of the oil. Stir in quinoa and beans. Remove from heat and set aside.

3. Drizzle remaining oil over bottom of baking dish. Set aside.

4. With tip of sharp knife, cut 1-inch (2.5 cm) diameter circle around stem of each pepper and discard the stem.

5. With spoon, carefully remove seeds from each, leaving remaining pepper intact. Transfer, open side up, to baking dish.

6. Carefully fill with salsa mixture. Evenly sprinkle cheese overtop.

7. Bake in oven until peppers are tender, about 30 minutes.

8. Garnish with cilantro.

Makes 4 servings

VEGETARIAN

MEXICAN

Three-Pepper Chicken
Fajitas

INGREDIENTS

- [ ] 3 or 4 boneless skinless chicken breasts, sliced thin
- [ ] 4 tbsp (60 mL) olive oil, divided
- [ ] 2 tbsp (30 mL) lime juice
- [ ] 1 tsp (5 mL) ground cumin
- [ ] 1 tsp (5 mL) garlic powder
- [ ] 1 tsp (5 mL) onion powder
- [ ] 1 onion, sliced in rings
- [ ] 1 sweet yellow pepper, sliced
- [ ] 1 sweet red pepper, sliced
- [ ] 1 sweet green pepper, sliced
- [ ] 8 flour tortillas, warmed (see TIP below)
- [ ] Store-bought salsa, for topping
- [ ] Non-fat Greek yogurt or sour cream, for garnish
- [ ] 1 or 2 limes, cut in wedges

Fajitas that sizzle on a cast-iron pan are surprisingly easy to make at home. Preheat a cast-iron pan in the oven with the tortillas (then remove the tortillas and wrap in a tea towel to keep warm) and enjoy the sizzle of the hot pan when you drop in the peppers and chicken right before serving.

1. In large resealable plastic bag, combine chicken, 2 tbsp (30 mL) of the oil, lime juice, cumin, garlic powder and onion powder.

2. Use your hands to gently move the chicken around inside the bag to coat it in the oil and spices. Seal and refrigerate for 20 minutes to marinate.

3. On an indoor or outdoor grill over medium-high heat, grill chicken until cooked through and no longer pink in centre, about 2 minutes per side, depending on the thickness of the slices.

4. Meanwhile, in non-stick saucepan or frying pan over medium-high heat add remaining oil.

5. Toss in the onion, yellow pepper, red pepper and green pepper. Sauté until tender-crisp, about 4 minutes.

6. Divide chicken and onion mixture evenly among tortillas; top with salsa and yogurt. Serve with lime wedges on side.

Makes 4 servings of 2 fajitas

> **TIP:**
> To warm tortillas, wrap in foil and bake in 250°F (120°C) oven for 15 minutes or wrap with damp paper towel and microwave for 30 to 60 seconds.

MEXICAN

BBQ Chicken, Jalapeño &

Avocado Quesadilla

INGREDIENTS

- [ ] 2 boneless, skinless chicken breasts, thinly sliced
- [ ] 4 cloves garlic, minced
- [ ] 2 tbsp (30 mL) olive oil
- [ ] 2 tbsp (30 mL) lime juice
- [ ] 4 large wheat tortillas
- [ ] 1 avocado, diced
- [ ] 1 jalapeño pepper, seeded and thinly sliced
- [ ] 1 cup (250 mL) Monterey Jack or colby cheese
- [ ] 1/4 cup (60 mL) chopped fresh cilantro + more, for garnish

SAUCE

- [ ] 1/2 cup (125 mL) sour cream
- [ ] 2 tbsp (30 mL) store-bought barbecue sauce

VARIATIONS:

If you are feeding a crowd, keep the assembled quesadillas warm in a 200°F (95°C) until serving.

These also make fantastic finger-food appetizers: simply slice into triangles, then top each with a teaspoon of sour cream and a cilantro leaf.

This is a perfect quick meal for one or for a crowd. Adjust the amount of jalapeño pepper to your liking, sprinkling more overtop, if you like it hot.

1. Sauce: In small bowl, whisk sour cream with barbecue sauce until blended and smooth. Cover and refrigerate until ready to use.

2. In large bowl, toss together chicken, garlic, oil and lime juice to coat. Set aside for 5 minutes to marinate.

3. Scrape chicken mixture (including marinade) into large frying pan over medium-high heat. Cook, stirring, until chicken is cooked through; set aside.

4. Heat non-stick frying pan over medium heat. Place 1 tortilla in pan. Over one half of tortilla, spread about half of the chicken mixture and top with half each of the avocado, jalapeño, cheese and cilantro.

5. With spatula, fold empty half overtop. Cover and cook until tortilla is toasted and cheese is melted, 1 to 2 minutes.

6. Uncover and carefully turn over. Cover and cook for 1 to 2 minutes.

7. Transfer to plate. Garnish with sauce and garnish with cilantro to complete one quesadilla. Cut the quesadilla into 4 wedges. Repeat with remaining tortilla and ingredients.

Makes 4 servings

MEXICAN

Black Bean, Salsa &
Cheddar Stuffed Sweet Potatoes

VEGETARIAN

VEGAN

MEXICAN

INGREDIENTS

- ☐ 1 tsp (5 mL) olive oil
- ☐ ½ cup (125 mL) black beans, drained and rinsed
- ☐ ½ cup (125 mL) store-bought salsa
- ☐ 1 sweet potato
- ☐ ¼ cup (60 mL) shredded cheddar cheese
- ☐ 2 tbsp (30 mL) non-fat Greek yogurt
- ☐ 1 tbsp (15 mL) lime juice
- ☐ Sprigs fresh cilantro (optional)

When you've only got a few minutes to make a meal, this is the dish. Microwaving the potato saves time and the end result has all the components of a balanced and nutritious meal. Protein-rich and plant-based, this is an easy option that is sure to become a quick-to-cook staple in your kitchen.

1. In non-stick frying pan over medium-high heat, warm oil. Stir in beans and salsa and cook, stirring, until heated through, about 5 minutes.

2. With tongs, transfer sweet potato to serving bowl; with tip of knife, slice an "X" in top side and, with fork, peel back skin, then fluff flesh and make well for bean mixture.

3. Spoon bean mixture into sweet potato; top with cheese, yogurt, lime juice and cilantro (if using).

Makes 1 serving

VARIATION:
For a vegan version, skip the dairy products and use vegan sour cream or unflavoured cultured soy or coconut-based yogurt, and vegan cheese.

Classic Casseroles

Cheesy Chicken &
Broccoli Casserole

INGREDIENTS

- ☐ Cooking spray, for pan
- ☐ 4 boneless skinless chicken breasts, cut in bite-size chunks
- ☐ 1 can (10 oz/284 mL) low-sodium condensed cream of mushroom soup
- ☐ 1/2 cup (125 mL) non-fat Greek yogurt
- ☐ 1/2 cup (125 mL) light mayonnaise
- ☐ 2 tbsp (30 mL) lemon juice
- ☐ 3 cloves garlic, minced
- ☐ 1/2 onion, diced
- ☐ 2 cups (500 mL) broccoli florets
- ☐ 2 cups (500 mL) cooked quinoa
- ☐ 2 cups (500 mL) shredded cheddar cheese

Casseroles: made for sharing! But you could make this classic dish for friends or keep it all for yourself and reap the benefits of leftovers on busy days. The beauty of casseroles? Cook once and eat twice (or even more, in this case), because they make an easy microwaveable meal.

1. Preheat oven to 375°F (190°C).

2. Coat inside of glass or ceramic baking dish with cooking spray. Set aside.

3. In large bowl, stir together chicken, soup, yogurt, mayonnaise and lemon juice to coat; fold in garlic, onion, broccoli and quinoa. Scrape into baking dish in even layer; evenly sprinkle with cheese. Bake in oven until bubbling and golden brown, 40 to 60 minutes. Transfer to rack; let cool for 5 to 10 minutes before serving.

Makes 4 to 6 servings

VARIATIONS:
Replace cooked quinoa with other cooked starch or grains such as rice or egg noodles, diced sweet potato or squash.
Make a vegetarian version, with meatless "chicken" strips or sausage, instead of chicken breast.

MAKE AHEAD:
Assemble casserole, cover with plastic wrap and refrigerate for up to 3 days or freeze for up to 2 months. Cover and bake from frozen, adding 20 to 30 minutes to cooking time. Uncover during the last 10 to 15 minutes to brown the top.

VEGETARIAN

NORTH AMERICAN

vegetable-loaded Tuna
Noodle Casserole

INGREDIENTS

- [ ] Cooking spray, for baking dish
- [ ] 1 package (12 oz / 340 g) egg noodles, cooked, drained and rinsed in cold water
- [ ] 2 cans (each 6 oz / 170 g) tuna, drained
- [ ] 1/2 cup (125 mL) diced red onion
- [ ] 2 cups (500 mL) shredded white cheddar cheese, divided
- [ ] 1 cup (250 mL) frozen green peas
- [ ] 1 stalk celery, diced
- [ ] 1 cup (250 mL) chopped baby spinach
- [ ] 1 cup (250 mL) broccoli florets
- [ ] 1 cup (250 mL) diced carrots
- [ ] 2 cans (each 10 oz / 284 mL) condensed cream of celery soup
- [ ] 1 cup (250 mL) crushed potato chips
- [ ] Salt and pepper to taste

Between the creamy soup and crunchy potato chip topping, this dishes up loads of warm and wholesome ingredients.

1. Preheat oven to 425°F (220°C).

2. Coat inside of glass or ceramic baking dish with cooking spray. Set aside.

3. In large bowl, stir together noodles, tuna, onion, 1 cup (250 mL) of the cheese, peas, celery, spinach, broccoli, carrots and soup.

4. Scrape into baking dish in even layer; sprinkle with potato chips and remaining cheese.

5. Bake in oven until bubbling and golden, 15 to 20 minutes, then season with salt and pepper.

Makes 4 to 6 servings

NORTH AMERICAN

VARIATIONS:
Swap egg noodles with the same amount of cooked pasta or grain that you have on hand.
Make a vegetarian version by replacing tuna with 1 can (14 oz / 398 mL) kidney beans.

MAKE AHEAD:
Assemble casserole (reserving toppings), cover with plastic wrap and refrigerate for up to 3 days or freeze for up to 2 months. Add toppings, cover and bake from frozen, adding 20 to 30 minutes to cooking time. Uncover during the last 10 to 15 minutes to keep the toppings crisp.

spaghetti squash Casserole

INGREDIENTS

- [ ] Cooking spray, for pan
- [ ] 1 spaghetti squash (about 3 lb/1.35 kg)
- [ ] Salt and pepper to taste
- [ ] 1 tbsp (15 mL) olive oil
- [ ] 1 yellow onion, chopped
- [ ] 1 tbsp (15 mL) red wine vinegar
- [ ] 1 tbsp (15 mL) maple syrup
- [ ] 1 bag (15 oz/425 g) baby spinach
- [ ] 1 cup (250 mL) goat cheese

VARIATION:
Add cooked ground pork or turkey to the casserole to make it a more substantial meal.

ITALIAN

Everyone has seen a spaghetti squash, but few know what to do with it. This recipe makes great use of this super-nutritious vegetable that soaks up delicious sauce just like pasta.

1. Preheat oven to 400°F (200°C).

2. Coat inside of glass or ceramic baking dish with cooking spray; set aside.

3. With sharp knife, trim and discard squash ends. Cut squash into 1-inch (2.5 cm) rings.

4. With bowl of spoon, scoop out and discard seeds from rings. Sprinkle all over with salt and pepper.

5. Transfer to parchment paper–lined rimmed baking sheet.

6. Bake in oven until tender, 20 to 30 minutes.

7. Transfer to rack. Let cool (leave oven on for casserole).

8. In non-stick frying pan over medium-high heat, warm oil. Add onion, reduce heat to medium-low and cook, stirring occasionally, until deep golden and fragrant, about 5 to 6 minutes.

9. Stir in vinegar and maple syrup; cook, scraping up brown bits from bottom of pan, for 2 minutes.

10. Remove from heat. Toss in spinach and half of the cheese until spinach is wilted and coated.

11. With hands, peel off and discard skin from squash and separate strands. Gently stir into onion mixture in pan.

12. With tongs, transfer to baking dish. Evenly sprinkle remaining cheese overtop. Bake in oven until edges are beginning to crisp, 15 to 20 minutes.

Makes 4 servings

Prep: 10 min | Cook: 45–60 min

Samosa Casserole

INGREDIENTS

- [ ] Cooking spray, for pan and phyllo sheets
- [ ] 3 potatoes, chopped
- [ ] 1/2 head cauliflower, chopped into florets
- [ ] 2 tbsp (30 mL) canola oil
- [ ] 1 yellow onion, diced
- [ ] 1 jalapeño pepper, seeded and minced
- [ ] 1-inch (2.5 cm) piece fresh ginger, minced
- [ ] 1 carrot, thinly sliced in rounds
- [ ] 2 tbsp (30 mL) curry powder
- [ ] 2 cups (500 mL) chopped spinach
- [ ] 1 cup (250 mL) frozen peas
- [ ] 1/4 cup (60 mL) chopped fresh cilantro
- [ ] 2 tbsp (30 mL) lemon juice
- [ ] 1 tsp (5 mL) salt
- [ ] 5 sheets phyllo pastry

VARIATION:
Add 1 lb (450 g) ground meat, 14 oz (398 mL) tofu or chickpeas to this dish to boost protein and make it a complete meal.

Samosas are those yummy deep-fried Indian pastries filled with savoury spiced vegetables, and sometimes meat. Although they are absolutely delish, their thick pastry soaks up oil like a sponge, making them not only tedious to make, but not-so-healthy, either. Samosa casserole preserves the spicy warmth of this popular street food but is far less time-consuming and far more heart-healthy.

1. Preheat oven to 375°F (190°C).

2. Coat inside of glass or ceramic baking dish with cooking spray. Set aside.

3. In large pot of boiling salted water, cook potatoes and cauliflower until tender.

4. Meanwhile, in non-stick frying pan over medium-high heat warm oil. Sauté onion, jalapeño and ginger until tender and fragrant, about 3-4 minutes.

5. Stir in carrot and curry powder. Sauté for 1 minute. Toss in spinach until wilted.

6. In large bowl, gently toss together potato mixture, onion mixture, peas, cilantro, lemon juice and salt.

7. Scrape into baking dish, firmly packing into even layer.

8. Coat 1 phyllo sheet all over with cooking spray.

9. With hands, pick up sheet and crumple (as you would a sheet of paper), then place on filling in dish. Repeat with remaining sheets to cover filling.

10. Bake in oven until phyllo is crisp and golden brown, about 30 minutes.

11. Transfer to rack. Let cool 5 to 10 minutes before serving.

Makes 6 servings

VEGETARIAN

VEGAN

INDIAN

Tex-Mex Chicken
CASSEROLE

INGREDIENTS

- [ ] Cooking spray, for pan
- [ ] 1 1/2 cups (325 mL) uncooked brown rice
- [ ] 1 can (14 oz/398 mL) black beans, drained and rinsed
- [ ] 1 can (14 oz/398 mL) corn kernels, drained
- [ ] 2 cups (500 mL) store-bought salsa
- [ ] 1 cup (250 mL) chicken stock
- [ ] 1 tbsp (15 mL) chili powder
- [ ] 2 to 3 boneless skinless chicken breasts, sliced
- [ ] 1 cup (250 mL) shredded cheddar cheese
- [ ] 1/4 cup (60 mL) chopped cilantro

Try serving this steamy casserole alongside a simple fresh salad of lettuce, tomato and avocado, drizzled with olive oil.

1. Preheat oven to 375°F (190°C).

2. Coat inside of glass or ceramic baking dish with cooking spray.

3. Stir in rice, beans, corn, salsa, chicken stock and chili powder.

4. Arrange chicken overtop, pressing into rice mixture. Wrap tightly with aluminum foil.

5. Bake in oven until rice is tender and cooked through, about 40 minutes.

6. Remove foil. Sprinkle cheese evenly overtop and cook just until cheese is bubbling.

7. Garnish with cilantro before serving.

Makes 4 to 6 servings

VARIATIONS:

To make your own faux sour cream to garnish each serving: Stir together 1 cup (250 mL) plain Greek yogurt, 2 tbsp (30 mL) lime juice and 1/2 tsp (2 mL) salt. Transfer any extra to airtight container and refrigerate for up to 7 to 10 days.

For a meatless version, use vegetarian sausage in place of the chicken.

Baked Garden Vegetables &
Tortellini

INGREDIENTS

- ☐ Cooking spray, for pan
- ☐ 1 1/2 cups (375 mL) chopped red pepper
- ☐ 1 1/2 cups (375 mL) chopped zucchini
- ☐ 1 cup (250 mL) sliced mushrooms
- ☐ 1 package (19 oz/500 g) tortellini, cooked, drained and rinsed in cold water

SAUCE

- ☐ 2 tbsp (30 mL) butter
- ☐ 1 tbsp (30 mL) all-purpose flour
- ☐ 3 cloves garlic, minced
- ☐ 1/2 onion, diced
- ☐ 2 cups (500 mL) milk
- ☐ 1 cup (250 mL) shredded mozzarella cheese, divided
- ☐ Salt and pepper to taste

Try swapping out the veggies and using up what you have on hand. This forgiving casserole is super-filling, and the carbohydrates make it great for physically demanding days.

1. Preheat oven to 400°F (200°C).

2. Coat inside of glass or ceramic baking dish with cooking spray. Set aside.

3. In bowl, toss together red pepper, zucchini and mushrooms. Set aside.

4. Sauce: In small saucepan over medium-high heat, melt butter. Stir in flour and cook, stirring, until smooth paste forms, about 1 minute.

5. Whisk in garlic, onion and milk. Cook, whisking constantly, until thickened into sauce.

6. Stir in half of the cheese until melted.

7. Evenly spread half of the sauce in bottom of dish. Evenly top with tortellini, then red pepper mixture.

8. Repeat with remaining sauce, tortellini and red pepper mixture. Evenly sprinkle with remaining cheese.

9. Bake in oven until vegetables are tender, about 30 minutes, then season with salt and pepper.

Makes 6 servings

VEGETARIAN

ITALIAN

VARIATION:
For a meaty version, add leftover cooked chicken or sausage to the dish.

MAKE AHEAD:
Assemble casserole, cover with plastic wrap and refrigerate for up to 3 days or freeze for up to 2 months. To bake from frozen, cover and add 20 to 30 minutes to cooking time.

Creamy Chicken,
Cauliflower & Bacon Casserole

INGREDIENTS

- [ ] 6 slices bacon, chopped
- [ ] 2 boneless, skinless chicken breasts, sliced
- [ ] 1/2 head of cauliflower, chopped into small florets
- [ ] 1 yellow onion, diced
- [ ] 4 cloves garlic, minced
- [ ] 2 cups (500 mL) low-sodium chicken broth
- [ ] 1/2 tsp (3 mL) cornstarch
- [ ] 2 tbsp (30 mL) cold water from the tap
- [ ] 8 oz (225 g) sodium-reduced cream cheese, cubed
- [ ] 1/2 cup (125 mL) white cheddar cheese, shredded
- [ ] Salt & freshly ground black pepper

Delicious over pasta, or just on its own, this casserole is a comfort classic.

1. Preheat the oven to 400°F (200°C). Place chopped bacon in an oven-safe pan over medium heat. Fry the bacon until crisp, and use a slotted spoon to transfer to a paper towel–lined plate. Discard all but 1 tbsp (15 mL) of bacon fat in the pan, and use it to sauté the chicken, cauliflower, onion and garlic for about 4 to 5 minutes.

2. Pour in the chicken broth, and bring to a gentle simmer. Whisk together the cornstarch with the water, and whisk into the chicken mixture. Stir in the cubed cream cheese and reserved bacon, and sprinkle the cheese over top.

3. Bake for about 15 minutes, or until the cheese is melted and turning golden. Season with salt and pepper to taste and serve.

Makes 6 to 8 servings

MEDITERRANEAM

Beef Taco Casserole

INGREDIENTS

- [ ] 1 lb (500 g) extra-lean ground beef
- [ ] 1 tbsp (15 mL) chili powder
- [ ] 16 oz (454 g) canned refried beans
- [ ] 2 cups (500 mL) cheddar or Monterey Jack cheese, shredded and divided
- [ ] Cooking spray
- [ ] 2 cups (500 mL) low-sodium tortilla chips, broken
- [ ] 2 green onions, thinly slicedly
- [ ] 1 cup (250 mL) romaine lettuce, chopped
- [ ] 1 medium tomato, chopped
- [ ] ¼ cup (60 mL) cilantro, chopped (optional)

Beef taco casserole is for those times when you feel the need for something gooey and indulgent. Use extra-lean beef, reduced sodium tortilla chips and pile the veggies high to get all the satisfaction without the junk.

1. Brown the ground beef in a non-stick pan over medium-high heat, using the spoon to break it up. Once it's cooked through, drain the fat and return to the pan. Stir in the chili powder and set aside.

2. In a medium saucepan over medium heat, stir together the refried beans and 1 cup of the cheese. Remove from the heat once heated through.

3. Use cooking spray to generously grease an 8" x 8" (20cm x 20cm) casserole dish and place the broken chips across the bottom.

4. Pour the refried bean mixture over the chips, followed by the ground beef.. Sprinkle the remaining cheese and green onion over the beef and bake at 400°F (200°C) for 15 minutes or until the cheese is fully melted.

5. Remove the pan from the oven and top by sprinkling with the lettuce, tomato and optional cilantro.

Makes 4 to 6 servings

VARIATION:
Enjoy a meatless version by omitting the beef or using vegetarian ground round instead.

VEGETARIAN

TEX-MEX

Tomato, Kale &
WHITE BEAN CASSEROLE

INGREDIENTS

- [ ] 2 tbsp (30 mL) olive oil
- [ ] 1 yellow onion, diced
- [ ] 3 to 4 cloves garlic, minced
- [ ] 18 oz (540 mL) can white kidney (cannellini) beans
- [ ] 2 cups (500 mL) lacinato kale leaves, chopped
- [ ] 14 1/2 oz (430 mL) can fire-roasted tomatoes
- [ ] 2 tbsp (30 mL) balsamic vinegar
- [ ] 1/2 tbsp (7 mL) sugar
- [ ] 1/4 tsp (1 mL) dried oregano
- [ ] 1/4 tsp (1 mL) dried basil
- [ ] 1/2 tsp (1 mL) ground thyme
- [ ] 1/2 cup (125 mL) whole wheat bread crumbs
- [ ] 1/4 cup (60 mL) Parmesan cheese, grated

Whole wheat bread crumbs and sharp Parmesan hold up to the hearty beans and greens.

1. Heat an oven-safe pan over medium-high heat. At the same time, pre-heat the oven to 400°F (200°C) degrees.

2. Pour in oil, and sauté the onion and garlic for about 2 to 3 minutes or until fragrant and beginning to wilt.

3. Introduce the beans and the kale to the pan, continuing to sauté. Pour in the canned tomatoes, vinegar, sugar and spices and bring to a simmer for about 10 minutes to thicken some of the juices.

4. While the ingredients simmer, combine bread crumbs with Parmesan in a small bowl and reserve.

5. Once the sauce has reduced, remove the pan from the heat and sprinkle the cheese mixture evenly over the top. Bake for 10 minutes or until the bread crumbs toast to a golden brown.

Makes 6 to 8 servings

VEGETARIAN

MEDITERRANEAN

Oven Baked

RATATOUILLE

INGREDIENTS

- [ ] 1 tbsp (15 mL) olive oil
- [ ] 1 cup (250 mL) store-bought marinara sauce
- [ ] 2 small potatoes, diced
- [ ] 1 medium eggplant, cubed
- [ ] 2 medium zucchini, cubed
- [ ] 3 tomatoes, diced
- [ ] 4 cloves garlic, minced
- [ ] ¹/₂ tsp (5 mL) dried basil
- [ ] ¹/₂ tsp (5 mL) dried oregano
- [ ] ¹/₂ cup (125 mL) Parmesan cheese, grated
- [ ] ¹/₂ cup (125 mL) mozzarella cheese, shredded

Ratatouille is a popular Mediterranean dish that combines some of summer's best produce. Traditionalists would season and stew each vegetable separately before combining them, but we've simplified the process and made it a perfect make-ahead, vegetable-based dish to eat all week long.

1. Preheat the oven to 400°F (200°C) degrees.

2. Prepare a large pie dish or a small casserole dish by greasing it with the olive oil.

3. Spread roughly ¹/₄ cup (60 mL) of the marinara sauce on the bottom of the dish. Layer the sliced vegetables over the sauce in the order of potato, eggplant, zucchini and tomato.

4. Season the vegetables by sprinkling with garlic, basil, and oregano over top. Pour the remaining marinara sauce over top and use the back of a spoon to gently spread.

5. Sprinkle the cheeses evenly over top and bake for approximately 40 to 50 minutes, or until vegetables are tender and cheese is melted and golden.

Makes 6 to 8 servings

VEGETARIAN

MEDITERRANEAN

Tomato & Basil
QUINOA CAPRESE

INGREDIENTS

- ☐ 2 tbsp (30 mL) olive oil for the pan
- ☐ 1 cup (250 mL) store-bought pasta sauce
- ☐ 1 tbsp (15 mL) tomato paste
- ☐ ½ tsp (3 mL) crushed red pepper
- ☐ ¼ cup (60 mL) 35% cream
- ☐ ½ (125 mL) cup Parmesan, grated
- ☐ 1 cup (250 mL) mozzarella, shredded
- ☐ 2 small plum or Roma tomatoes, diced
- ☐ ½ cup (125 mL) fresh basil, chopped
- ☐ 2 cups (500 mL) cooked quinoa

VEGETARIAN

ITALIAN

Nutty quinoa brings a warm and hearty element to the classic flavours of summertime — tomato, basil and mozzarella salads. I suggest serving this with a sunny-side egg placed delicately on top as a classy brunch dish.

1. Preheat oven to 450°F (230°C). Grease a casserole dish with the olive oil and set aside.

2. Heat a medium saucepan over medium-high heat and stir together the pasta sauce, tomato paste and crushed red pepper.

3. Stir in the cream, Parmesan and half of the mozzarella. Add the tomatoes and stir to heat through.

4. Remove from the heat and stir in most of the basil. Spread the quinoa into the prepared pan, spread the tomato sauce over top and sprinkle with remaining mozzarella and basil.

5. Bake for 5 to 10 minutes or until cheese is melted and golden.

Makes 4 servings

The sweet stuff

peanut Butter &
Chocolate Chunk Cookies

INGREDIENTS

- [ ] 1 can (14 oz/398 mL) chickpeas, drained and rinsed
- [ ] 1/2 cup (125 mL) natural peanut butter
- [ ] 1/4 cup (60 mL) liquid honey or agave
- [ ] 2 tsp (10 mL) vanilla extract
- [ ] 1 tsp (5 mL) baking powder
- [ ] Pinch salt
- [ ] 1/2 cup (125 mL) chocolate chunks

I could barely believe my taste buds when I tried this: chickpeas are the secret ingredient that make these cookies ultracreamy and melty. Serve a little warm. (and don't bother telling people about the chickpeas — they will never know the difference).

1. Preheat oven to 350°F (180°C).

2. In food processor, purée chickpeas, peanut butter, honey or agave, vanilla, baking powder and salt until blended and smooth.

3. Fold in chocolate chunks.

4. With moistened hands, form 2 tbsp (30 mL) balls.

5. Transfer to parchment paper–lined baking sheet. With moistened tines of fork, gently press each to flatten.

6. Bake in oven for 10 minutes; serve warm.

Makes 16 cookies

> **TIP:**
> Microwave leftover cookies for 15 to 30 seconds to rewarm.

VEGETARIAN

VEGAN

NORTH AMERICAN

peanut & marshmallow
DARK CHOCOLATE FUDGE

INGREDIENTS

- [ ] 1 1/2 cups (375 mL) dark chocolate chips, divided
- [ ] 1 cup (250 mL) unsalted roasted peanut pieces, divided
- [ ] 1 cup (250 mL) miniature marshmallows, divided
- [ ] 1 cup (250 mL) crispy rice cereal
- [ ] 3 tbsp (45 mL) icing sugar
- [ ] 1/2 cup (125 mL) evaporated milk

Crunchy peanuts, chewy marshmallows and a dark chocolate fudge layer on top = pure bliss. This is a great snack for kids and adults alike.

1. Into bowl, transfer 2 tbsp (30 mL) each of the chocolate chips, peanuts and marshmallows. Toss in cereal and icing sugar. Set aside.

2. In heatproof bowl, microwave remaining chocolate chips and milk on high in 15-second increments, stirring between each, until chocolate is melted and blended.

3. With spatula, gently fold two-thirds of the melted mixture into chocolate-chip mixture to coat.

4. Scrape into parchment paper–lined 8-inch (20 cm) square baking pan, pressing into even layer.

5. Spread remaining melted mixture overtop; sprinkle with remaining chocolate-chip mixture, pressing into bottom layer.

6. Cover and refrigerate until firm and set, 1 to 2 hours. Cut into 16 squares.

Makes 16 servings

VARIATION:
If preferred, replace the peanuts with broken pecans and almonds, and substitute crushed pretzels for the cereal.

VEGETARIAN

NORTH AMERICAN

Dark Chocolate,
Cranberry & Pretzel Bark

INGREDIENTS

- [ ] 6 oz (170 g) dark or semisweet chocolate, coarsely chopped
- [ ] $1/3$ cup (75 mL) coarsely broken pretzels
- [ ] 2 tbsp (30 mL) dried sweetened cranberries
- [ ] Coarse salt to taste

This is a super-easy dessert that's great for an informal get-together or easily packaged as a gift. Try varying the fruit and swapping your favourite nuts for the pretzels, but keep the dark chocolate instead of milk chocolate, because it's higher in antioxidants, lower in sugar and has been shown to have beneficial effects on heart and brain health.

1. Line rimmed baking sheet with parchment paper. Set aside.

2. In heatproof bowl, microwave chocolate on high in 30-second increments, stirring between each, until melted.

3. With spatula, scrape into pan and evenly spread.

4. Sprinkle pretzels, cranberries and salt evenly overtop, gently pressing into chocolate.

5. Let stand at room temperature for 1 to 2 hours or cover and freeze for 10 minutes. Break into chunks.

Makes 6 servings

VARIATION:
Try using different dried fruit and nut combinations such as dried pineapple with macadamia nuts, banana chips and peanuts, or raisins and walnuts.

VEGETARIAN

VEGAN

NORTH AMERICAN

Crunchy fruit &
Seed Oatmeal Cookies

INGREDIENTS

- [ ] 1 egg
- [ ] 1/2 cup (125 mL) butter, softened
- [ ] 1/2 cup (125 mL) packed brown sugar
- [ ] 1/2 cup (125 mL) applesauce
- [ ] 1 tsp (5 mL) almond or vanilla extract
- [ ] 1 cup (250 mL) whole wheat flour
- [ ] 1 cup (250 mL) large-flake rolled oats
- [ ] 1/2 cup (125 mL) dried cranberries
- [ ] 1/2 cup (125 mL) raw sunflower seeds
- [ ] 1/2 cup (125 mL) raw pumpkin seeds
- [ ] 1/2 cup (125 mL) wheat germ
- [ ] 1/4 cup (60 mL) sesame seeds
- [ ] 1/4 cup (60 mL) ground flaxseed
- [ ] 1 tsp (5 mL) baking soda
- [ ] 1/2 tsp (2 mL) salt
- [ ] 1/2 tsp (2 mL) cinnamon

These cookies are so wholesome they can double as breakfast. Dunk them into hot tea or a glass of your favourite cold milk.

1. Preheat oven to 375°F (190°C).

2. In bowl, beat egg, butter, brown sugar, applesauce and almond extract together until blended and creamy.

3. In large bowl, toss together flour, oats, cranberries, sunflower seeds, pumpkin seeds, wheat germ, sesame seeds, flaxseed, baking soda, salt and cinnamon.

4. Stir in egg mixture until thoroughly mixed.

5. About 1 tbsp (15 mL) at a time, drop onto parchment paper–lined baking sheet, 2-inch (5-cm) apart.

6. Bake in oven until edges are crisp and golden, 10 to 15 minutes.

7. Let cool in pan on rack for 5 minutes. With spatula, transfer to rack. Let cool.

Makes 16 cookies

VEGETARIAN

SCOTTISH

> **VARIATION:**
> For truly decadent cookies, use same amount of dark chocolate chips instead of cranberries.

Chocolate & peanut Butter
Rice Treats

VEGETARIAN

VEGAN

NORTH AMERICAN

INGREDIENTS

- ☐ ¹/₂ cup + 1 tbsp (125 mL + 15 mL) natural peanut butter, divided
- ☐ ¹/₂ cup (125 mL) liquid honey or agave syrup
- ☐ 1 tsp (5 mL) vanilla extract
- ☐ Pinch salt
- ☐ 3 cups (750 mL) puffed rice cereal
- ☐ 1 package (8 oz / 250 g) semisweet chocolate chips

Even though these beauties contain little to no refined sugar, they are still absolutely mouth watering. You earn bonus healthy points for using crisped brown-rice cereal and you won't even notice the difference.

1. In large saucepan over medium heat, melt ¹/₂ cup (125 mL) of the peanut butter, honey, vanilla and salt, whisking constantly, until blended and smooth. Stir in rice cereal to coat.

2. Scrape into parchment paper–lined 8-inch (20 cm) square pan, spreading evenly.

3. In small heatproof bowl, microwave remaining peanut butter and chocolate chips in 20-second increments, stirring between each, until melted and blended.

4. Spread over peanut butter mixture in pan.

5. Cover and refrigerate until firm and set, about 30 minutes. Slice into 16 squares.

Makes 16 squares

Chocolate Avocado
PUDDING

INGREDIENTS

- [ ] 4 oz (115 g) dark chocolate, coarsely chopped
- [ ] 4 ripe Hass avocados, halved and diced
- [ ] ¹/₂ cup (125 mL) agave syrup or liquid honey
- [ ] ¹/₃ cup (75 mL) almond, coconut, macadamia or cashew nut milk
- [ ] 2 tsp (10 mL) vanilla extract
- [ ] ¹/₂ cup (125 mL) cocoa powder
- [ ] ¹/₂ tsp (2 mL) salt
- [ ] ¹/₄ cup (60 mL) raspberries (optional)
- [ ] 2 tbsp (30 mL) hazelnut flakes (optional)

The healthy fat and fibre found in avocados, paired with antioxidant-rich cocoa, makes this dessert super-nutritious. Try serving this mousse right in the avocado skins with a few nuts or chopped fruit sprinkled on top.

1. In heatproof bowl, microwave chocolate in 15-second increments, stirring between each, until melted; set aside.

2. In food processor, purée avocados, agave syrup, almond milk and vanilla for a few seconds.

3. Add chocolate; pulse for 30 to 45 seconds to combine.

4. Scrape down side, add cocoa powder and salt; purée, scraping down side once or twice, until blended and smooth.

5. Divide evenly among 4 serving bowls; garnish with raspberries and hazelnut flakes (if using).

Makes 4 servings

VARIATIONS:
- Replace nut milk with the same amount of cold coffee.
- Add a few slices of banana with a spoonful or two of peanut butter.
- Substitute half of the vanilla extract for mint extract and garnish with fresh mint leaves.

TIP:
If you want to save the avocado skins for "serving dishes," use bowl of large spoon to scoop flesh from avocado skin.

VEGETARIAN

VEGAN

NORTH AMERICAN

Best Banana
MUFFINS

INGREDIENTS

- [ ] Cooking spray, for pan
- [ ] 3 fresh or thawed frozen bananas
- [ ] 1 egg
- [ ] ¹/₂ cup (125 mL) non-fat yogurt
- [ ] ¹/₄ cup (60 mL) liquid honey
- [ ] 1 tbsp (15 mL) vanilla extract
- [ ] 1 cup (250 mL) whole wheat flour
- [ ] ¹/₄ cup (60 mL) ground flaxseed
- [ ] 1 tsp (5 mL) baking soda
- [ ] ¹/₂ tsp (2 mL) cinnamon
- [ ] ¹/₂ cup (125 mL) mini semisweet chocolate chips

Straight out of the oven, these will put you in a trance, but they might be even better when you've stashed a few in the freezer and can grab one as you're running out the door. Store ripe bananas in the freezer to defrost when you need them; With a slice across the top, the banana pulp will easily slip out of the skin.

1. Preheat oven to 350°F (180°C).

2. Coat 12-cup muffin tin with cooking spray. Set aside.

3. In food processer or blender, purée bananas, egg, yogurt, honey and vanilla until blended and smooth.

4. In bowl, whisk flour, flaxseed, baking soda and cinnamon. Stir in banana mixture just until combined. Fold in chocolate chips.

5. Divide batter among muffin cups.

6. Bake in oven until puffed and centres spring back when gently pressed, about 20 minutes.

Makes 12 muffins

> **VARIATION:**
> Replace chocolate chips with same amount of blueberries or walnut pieces.

VEGETARIAN

NORTH AMERICAN

pumpkin pie
SMOOTHIE

INGREDIENTS

- [ ] ³/₄ cup (175 mL) pumpkin purée
- [ ] 1 soft ripe banana
- [ ] 1 cup (250 mL) milk or unsweetened nondairy milk
- [ ] 1 tbsp (15 mL) liquid honey
- [ ] 1 tsp (5 mL) pumpkin pie spice (³/₄ tsp/4 mL cinnamon + ¹/₄ tsp/1 mL ground ginger + 1/4 tsp/1 mL nutmeg)
- [ ] ¹/₂ tsp (2 mL) vanilla extract
- [ ] 5 or 6 ice cubes

Canned pumpkin purée is a great thing to keep on hand, if only for this smoothie that's as satisfying for breakfast on a hot summer day as it is for a fall dessert. Refrigerate or freeze any extra pumpkin purée in resealable freezer bags for future smoothies.

1. In food processor or blender, purée pumpkin, banana, milk, honey, pumpkin pie spice, vanilla and ice cubes; serve immediately.

Makes 2 servings

VARIATION:
Add 1 or 2 spoonfuls of yogurt to increase the protein and bring this smoothie from a dessert to a meal.

VEGETARIAN

VEGAN

NORTH AMERICAN

Banana split
SMOOTHIE

INGREDIENTS

- [ ] 1 fresh or thawed frozen banana
- [ ] 1 cup (250 mL) milk or unsweetened nondairy milk
- [ ] $1/2$ cup (125 mL) fresh or frozen strawberries + more for garnish (optional)
- [ ] $1/2$ cup (125 mL) fresh, frozen or drained canned pineapple chunks + more for garnish (optional)
- [ ] 5 or 6 ice cubes
- [ ] 2 tbsp (30 mL) store-bought chocolate sauce, divided
- [ ] 1 tbsp (15 mL) salted peanut pieces (optional)

This childhood favourite is transformed into a nutritious smoothie that's perfect for an adult. Prepare to bliss out.

1. In food processor or blender, purée banana, milk, strawberries, pineapple and ice cubes.

2. Transfer to serving glass. Fold in 1 tbsp (15 mL) of the chocolate sauce to create swirl.

3. Drizzle remaining chocolate sauce over top. Garnish with strawberries, pineapple and/or peanuts (if using).

Makes 1 serving

VARIATION:
Use chocolate or vanilla-flavoured milk to make this smoothie extra-decadent.

VEGETARIAN

VEGAN

NORTH AMERICAN

Mint & Chocolate Chip
SMOOTHIE

INGREDIENTS

- [ ] 1 cup (250 mL) loosely packed baby spinach leaves
- [ ] 1 cup (250 mL) milk or unsweetened nondairy milk
- [ ] ³/₄ cup (175 mL) non-fat Greek yogurt
- [ ] ¹/₄ cup (60 mL) packed mint leaves
- [ ] 1 tbsp (15 mL) liquid honey
- [ ] 5 or 6 ice cubes
- [ ] 2 tbsp (30 mL) mini dark chocolate chips, divided

This tastes just like Girl Guide cookies ... need I say more?

1. In food processor or blender, purée spinach, milk, yogurt, mint, honey, ice cubes and half of the chocolate chips.

2. Divide evenly between 2 serving glasses; garnish with remaining chocolate chips.

Makes 2 servings

VEGETARIAN

NORTH AMERICAN

strawberry Cheesecake
SMOOTHIE

INGREDIENTS

- [ ] 2 graham crackers, coarsely broken
- [ ] ³/₄ cup (175 mL) frozen strawberries
- [ ] ³/₄ cup (175 mL) milk or unsweetened nondairy milk
- [ ] ¹/₂ fresh or thawed frozen banana
- [ ] ¹/₂ cup (125 mL) vanilla Greek yogurt
- [ ] 2 tbsp (30 mL) cream cheese
- [ ] 1 tbsp (15 mL) liquid honey

As dessert or just an indulgent breakfast, this smoothie is as good as the real deal. Try upping the fancy ante by rimming the glass in graham cracker crumbs for guests.

1. In food processor or blender, pulse graham crackers until in coarse crumbs.

2. Transfer to small bowl and set aside.

3. In food processor or blender, purée strawberries, milk, banana, yogurt, cheese, and honey until blended and smooth.

4. Transfer to serving glass; garnish with graham cracker crumbs.

Makes 1 serving

VARIATION:
Use vanilla-flavoured milk and half of the honey for another delightful version of this smoothie.

VEGETARIAN

NORTH AMERICAN

Chocolate-Covered
Banana Bites

INGREDIENTS

- ☐ 2 small bananas, thickly sliced (about 8 slices per banana)
- ☐ 1 cup (250 mL) dark chocolate chips
- ☐ 1 tbsp (15 mL) coconut oil

Super-yummy banana bites are a dream to whip up — and they please the fanciest of guests or the grubbiest of kids (sometimes both at the same time). Serve them on their own or over a bowl of ice cream for maximum impact.

1. Arrange banana slices in single layer on parchment paper–lined rimmed baking sheet that fits flat in your freezer. Freeze for 5 to 10 minutes.

2. Meanwhile, in small heatproof bowl, microwave chocolate chips and coconut oil in 15-second increments, stirring between each, until melted and blended.

3. With tongs, gently dip each banana slice into chocolate mixture to coat all over, then return to baking sheet. Return pan to freezer until firm and set, about 5 to 10 minutes.

Makes 16 bites

VARIATIONS:
- To lighten this up, dip just half of each banana slice into the melted chocolate.
- To make these even more luxurious, sandwich a scoop of your favourite nut butter between two banana slices before dipping them into the melted chocolate.

MAKE AHEAD:
Transfer frozen bites into parchment paper–lined plastic tub, cover and freeze for up to 2 weeks, for a sweet treat that's ready when you are.

VEGETARIAN

VEGAN

NORTH AMERICAN

Strawberries

INGREDIENTS

- ☐ 1 cup (250 mL) dark chocolate chips
- ☐ 1 tbsp (15 mL) coconut oil
- ☐ About 20 large strawberries, patted dry with paper towel
- ☐ Toothpicks, for dipping

There's a reason that celebrations from wedding receptions to Super Bowl parties have these on the menu. Try serving this easy make-ahead dessert in fancy mini-muffin liners to a crowd.

1. In small heatproof bowl, microwave chocolate chips and coconut oil in 15-second increments, stirring between each, until melted and blended.

2. Piercing each strawberry with toothpick 'handle," dip strawberries, one at a time, into melted chocolate; transfer to parchment paper–lined rimmed baking sheet or tray.

3. Refrigerate until firm and set, about 5-6 minutes. Remove toothpicks before serving.

Makes 20 strawberries

VARIATION:
While chocolate coating is still warm, sprinkle with shredded coconut or your favourite finely crushed nuts or cookies.

MAKE AHEAD:
Transfer to airtight container and refrigerate for up to 2 days.

VEGETARIAN

VEGAN

ITALIAN

Blender Banana
Ice Cream

INGREDIENTS

☐ 1 soft ripe banana, sliced in rounds

Bananas magically transform into a creamy custardy sweet ice cream just by freezing and blending them. It's really that simple, but, if you want a bit of pizzazz, try adding one of the flavour combinations, below.

1. In airtight container or resealable freezer bag, freeze banana for at least 1 hour or overnight.

2. Transfer to food processor; pulse, stopping to scrape down side, just until blended and smooth.

3. Evenly divide between 2 serving bowls; serve immediately.

Makes 2 servings

> **VARIATIONS:**
> • Purée with 1 tbsp (15 mL) peanut or coconut butter.
> • Fold in 2 tbsp (30 mL) chocolate chips, nuts or chopped dried fruit before serving.
> • Purée with 1/4 tsp (1 mL) cinnamon, ground ginger, or vanilla or almond extract.

VEGETARIAN

VEGAN

ITALIAN

Coffee-Cup Cakes,
Crisps & Cobblers

INGREDIENTS

DOUBLE CHOCOLATE BROWNIE

- ☐ 2 tbsp (30 mL) butter, melted
- ☐ 2 tbsp (30 mL) water
- ☐ 1/2 tsp (2 mL) vanilla extract
- ☐ Dash salt
- ☐ 2 tbsp (30 mL) cocoa powder
- ☐ 3 tbsp (45 mL) white sugar
- ☐ 1/4 cup (60 mL) all-purpose flour
- ☐ 1 tbsp (15 mL) semisweet chocolate chips

LEMON CAKE

- ☐ 1 large egg
- ☐ 2 tbsp (30 mL) vegetable oil
- ☐ 2 tsp (10 mL) lemon juice, divided
- ☐ 3 tbsp (45 mL) all-purpose flour
- ☐ 1/4 tsp (1 mL) baking powder
- ☐ 1 tsp (5 mL) lemon zest
- ☐ 3 tbsp (45 mL) white sugar
- ☐ 1 tbsp (15 mL) icing sugar

We know that we single people are supposed to only portion out one or two cookies from the batch of dough and freeze the rest, but who actually does that? Nobody. So here's the solution: quick cooking and portion-controlled sweets for when the craving strikes.

DOUBLE CHOCOLATE BROWNIE

Whisk together the butter, water, vanilla and salt in a large coffee mug. Gradually whisk in the cocoa, followed by the sugar, and then the flour. Microwave for 1 1/2 minutes, until the centre is still slightly molten in texture. Sprinkle chocolate chips over top and enjoy.

Makes 1 mug brownie

LEMON CAKE

Spray a large coffee mug with cooking spray and set aside. In a small bowl, whisk together the egg, oil, and 1 tsp (5 mL) of the juice. Gradually whisk in the flour, baking powder, lemon zest and sugar into the wet ingredients. Pour into the prepared mug and microwave on high for 1 1/2 minutes. While the cake microwaves, whisk together the remaining lemon juice with the icing sugar. Allow the cake to cool in the mug. Once the cake has cooled, drizzle glaze over top to serve.

Makes 1 mug cake

VEGETARIAN

NORTH AMERICAN

APPLE CRISP

- [ ] 1 apple, grated
- [ ] 2 tbsp (30 mL) brown sugar
- [ ] 2 tbsp (30 mL) quick oats
- [ ] 1 tbsp (15 mL) all-purpose flour
- [ ] 1 tbsp (15 mL) butter
- [ ] $^1/_4$ tsp cinnamon

BERRY COBBLER

- [ ] $^3/_4$ cup (180 mL) mixed berries (fresh or frozen)
- [ ] 2 tbsp (30 mL) brown sugar
- [ ] 2 tbsp (30 mL) quick oats
- [ ] 1 tbsp (15 mL) all-purpose flour
- [ ] 1 tbsp (15 mL) butter
- [ ] $^1/_4$ tsp (1 mL) cinnamon

APPLE CRISP

Prepare a large coffee mug with a quick mist of cooking spray. Place the grated apple in the bottom of the mug. In a small bowl, use a fork to crumble together the brown sugar, oats, flour, butter and cinnamon. Carefully pour the crumbled mixture over top the apple inside the mug. Microwave on high for 2 to 2 $^1/_2$ minutes.

Makes 1 mug crisp

BERRY COBBLER

Prepare a large coffee mug with a quick mist of cooking spray. Place the berries in the bottom of the mug. In a small bowl, use a fork to crumble together the brown sugar, oats, flour, butter and cinnamon. Carefully pour the crumbled mixture over top the berries inside the mug. Microwave on high for 2 to 2 $^1/_2$ minutes.

Makes 1 mug cobbler

VEGETARIAN

NORTH AMERICAN

Middle Eastern
BAKED PEARS

INGREDIENTS

- ☐ 4 Bartlett pears, halved and cored
- ☐ 2 tbsp (30 mL) water
- ☐ 2 tbsp (30 mL) butter, melted
- ☐ 2 tbsp (30 mL) liquid honey
- ☐ 1/2 tsp (2 mL) cinnamon
- ☐ 1/4 cup (60 mL) walnuts or pistachio pieces
- ☐ 2 cups (500 mL) Greek yogurt

If you like the sweet flavours of fruit instead of full-bodied chocolate for dessert, this is for you. But try grating a bit of chocolate overtop for anyone who likes it rich.

1. Preheat oven to 400°F (200°C).

2. In small baking dish, arrange pears, cut-side down; pour in water.

3. Drizzle with butter and honey and sprinkle cinnamon overtop.

4. Bake in oven, basting then sprinkling walnuts into pan between pears halfway through, until pears are tender, about 20 minutes.

5. Remove from heat and transfer pears to serving dishes. Let cool for 1 to 2 minutes.

6. Top each with scoop of yogurt; drizzle with cooking syrup and sprinkle with walnuts from pan.

Makes 4 to 8 servings

VEGETARIAN

MIDDLE EASTERN

Index

MARQUIS

Québec, Canada